SENSING

THE *Spirit*

SENSING
THE *Spirit*

The Holy Spirit in
Feminist Perspective

Rebecca Button Prichard

Chalice Press
St. Louis, Missouri

All scripture quotations, unless otherwise indicated, are from the *New Revised Standard Version Bible*, copyright 1989, Division of Christian Education of the National Council of the Churches of Christ in the United States of America. Used by permission. All rights reserved.

The excerpt from Miriam Therese Winter, *WomanPrayer and WomanSong: Resources for Ritual*, is used with permission of The Crossroad Publishing Company.

Cover Design: Elizabeth Wright
Interior Design: Elizabeth Wright
Cover Art: "The Large Piece of Turf" by Albrecht Dürer, Graphische Sammlung, Albertina, Vienna. Used by permission.

This book is printed on acid-free, recycled paper.

Visit Chalice Press on the World Wide Web at
www.chalicepress.com

10 9 8 7 6 5 4 3 2 1   99 00 01 02 03

Library of Congress Cataloging–in–Publication Data

Prichard, Rebecca Button.
    Sensing the Spirit : the Holy Spitit in feminist perspective / by Rebecca Button Prichard.
        p.   cm.
    Includes bibliographical references and index.
    ISBN 0-8272-3442-2
    1. Holy Spirit. 2. Feminist theology. I. Title.
BT121.2.P75 1999
231'.3'082 — dc21   99-38561
                                                                CIP

Printed in the United States of America

To my parents

Contents

Preface

I began this book in the growing greenness of springtime. I've completed the final chapter in the bleak midwinter, snowed in, hunkered down. I'll surely be ready when spring comes 'round again, but the Spirit is perceptible in the snow and ice, too. Life is cyclical and circling, just so the Spirit's blowing circles and cycles 'round, like liturgical and academic seasons, comforting in their predictability, surprising in terms of newness.

This book seeks to fill a gap in the literature, there being no work of feminist theology I know of devoted primarily to reflection on the Holy Spirit. Naturally, I hope to provoke rather than end conversation on the subject. I expect there will be those among the systematic theologians who find my form too free, my content too concrete. Some feminists may find my approach too trusting, too traditional. I am well aware that my particular weaving together of scripture, church history, and spirituality is drawn from my own social, ecclesiastical, and cultural location. My goal is not to hold up my usable past as a norm, but to urge others to patch together usable snippets of history and tradition that illuminate their lives in the Spirit.

Many of my conversation partners are named in the footnotes of this book; others are remembered in the anecdotal passages. Souls for whom I've cared as a pastor in California and Indiana and Scotland have had a part. Seminary students in Indianapolis and Doctor of Ministry students in San Anselmo have contributed more than they know. Friends who have surrounded and supported me in good times and in fiery ordeal are present as well. Wherever I have been, there has always been a sisterhood, a group of kindred spirits who together have tried to keep the faith and who bear with me still. I acknowledge and thank you all, sisters and other wise ones.

Oddly enough, a handful of male colleagues have appointed themselves "midwives" or rather birthing coaches for this book, kidding, cajoling, cheering me on—Clark Williamson says there's nothing as exciting as birthing a book. Ron Allen says I'm limiting the Spirit's resourcefulness if I think men can't be midwives. Charles Allen has allowed me to borrow and play with his notion of eccentricity. And, of course, my parents call regularly from California to see if the book is finished yet (maybe because I've borne them no grandchildren). All in all, much better consolers than Job's cohort.

If males can encourage a feminist theologian, she must speak briefly but clearly about language. I refer to the Holy Spirit in female terms throughout this book. This is due primarily to the fact that the Bible rarely, if ever, uses masculine language for the Spirit; *ruach* is feminine, *pneuma* is neutral. But I want to argue with any feminization of the Spirit that seeks to define her only in relation to the Father and the Son, for this casts her as female according to the sensibilities of patriarchy. Jesus' humanity was undeniably a male humanity, and though I occasionally lift up traditions that speak of Christ in feminine language, I accept Jesus' maleness as particular to his incarnation but not as normative for salvation or for human beings in the image of God. I try to avoid pronouns in speaking of God, the Trinitarian person we call Father, Mother, Parent, Creator, not because I believe this God to be impersonal, but because I believe both male and female bear the image of this God and that God must transcend and embrace both gender and sexuality. I hope this helps to express the care with which I've tried to speak of God. I've usually chosen not to edit exclusive language out of other people's words, including the words of scripture. I look forward to the day when we no longer have to explain such things.

A former student asked me recently what it's like to be writing a book about the Holy Spirit. I took her to mean, "Do you sense the Spirit in your writing?" A daunting yet comforting question, for the project would be meaningless if I didn't notice the Spirit's presence from time to time, which, thankfully, I have. The most life-changing events in my life have come seemingly uninvited. The idea for this book was just a spark when Jon Berquist first spoke to me about it. He has been a most encouraging editor, urging me to let my voice be heard and confirming often the Spirit's prompting.

Epiphany 1999

Introduction

"The wind blows where it chooses; and you hear the sound of it, but you do not know where it comes from or where it goes" (Jn. 3:8). The spirit/wind has been blowing in my thinking and reading and preaching and teaching for some time now; only in retrospect do I see a kind of willfulness in her whispers. A series of Pentecost sermons, a lecture here, an adult Sunday school lesson there, a seminary course on women mystics—in these and other reflective encounters the sound of the spirit/wind has been heard, at first glance, without rhyme or reason.

Only when I set out to compile a bibliography of women working in systematic theology did I notice the gaping lacuna in the literature. As far as I could tell, no feminist theologian had written a book-length study on the doctrine of the Holy Spirit.[1] As I looked more closely, I noted that even those women who had written theological systems loosely based on the classic *loci* seemed to skip over pneumatology or to translate it into spirituality.[2] My sense of wonder increased as I noted the appearance in recent years of a number of significant pneumatologies and the flurry of interest in the Holy Spirit surrounding the Canberra Assembly of the World Council of Churches.[3]

A Pentecost Bible study for a church in California first drew me into the very sensual language that scripture uses to portray Spirit. I was struck by the way biblical images for the Holy Spirit—tongues of flame, mighty wind, fiery pillar, new wine—appeal to the senses. This seemed a direct contrast to the way theology usually portrays Spirit—as invisible, numinous, ghostly, intangible. As I searched scripture with an eye to sense-appealing images, a full-blown sensual pneumatology began to emerge.

1

Spiritual Theology

At the same time I became increasingly engaged in the study of the mystics. My doctoral work had introduced me to these writings. Mystical and spiritual writings seemed to be taught only at the margins of church history and seldom, if ever, as a source for systematic or constructive theological reflection. Further study made it clear that the spiritual writings of women mystics tend toward the concrete, whereas those male mystics who were also trained in theological reflection move much more quickly to abstraction.[4] Christian mystical writing, from the desert fathers onward, seemed to me to be concerned with the triumph of spirit over body. Indeed, this struggle appears to form a basis for the ascetic impulse in many religions.

Yet I noticed exceptions to this in many cases, especially in some of those earthy accounts offered by mystical women. Bodily, sensual images became a means of interpreting the spiritual, the ineffable.[5] While spiritual writing had been a primary mode of theological reflection in the early church, with the rise of the medieval universities, doctrinal genres took precedence.[6] Spiritual autobiography became an alternate and subordinate form of theological reflection, based in the religious experience rather than the rational ruminations of the author. *Summae* and Sentences overshadowed Confessions and *Vitae*—at least in the academic realm. Since virtually all the texts written by women in this period were written in spiritual genres, women's exclusion from the theological mainstream was reinforced by the discounting of their texts.

Liturgical Theology

My own experience as a preacher, a teacher, a seminary professor, and a faithful Christian come into play in this study; so also my role as a liturgist. I have long noted that much Protestant worship is primarily cerebral, that words come in through our eyes and ears but that the five senses are hardly ever piqued as they are in Anglican, Roman Catholic, and Orthodox liturgy. The colors and the textures, the smells and the bells of so-called high church worship appeal in an aesthetic way to the intuition, the imagination, the inner soul of the worshiper. The Protestant reformations made much of the importance of understanding in their word-centered worship; the Enlightenment simply reinforced this emphasis. Over the years many of our mainline churches have embraced music, stained glass, liturgical colors, even dance and candles on occasion, but most Protestant worship is hardly what one would call "embodied" or "sensual," much less affirming of women's bodies.[7]

Reforming Feminism

And so *Sensing the Spirit* is a project that arises out of my own experiences as a Protestant, feminist pastor and scholar, a woman with varied interests and a passion for ongoing reformation. The right relation between body and spirit has been crucial to feminist scholars, including those working in the tradition of Christian theology.[8] The ascetic impulse of monasticism, which spills over into Protestantism, as well as the abstract approach of academic theology, have promoted and entrenched the divide between the material and spiritual realms, and between bodies, minds, and spirits. As feminists have pointed out, maleness has become associated with those spiritual and intellectual pursuits that seek to transcend the limitations of embodied experience, naturally associated with carnal, earthy femaleness.[9] Mary Gray speaks of this dualism with regard to pneumatology:

> The life of the Spirit is seen to be more authentically male, and the link between women and all that is "natural," bodily, physical and "earthy" is interpreted as impediment to their attaining the heights of holiness. An even more serious implication is that the life of the Spirit—because "pure Spirit" has no contact with matter—is that which directs us away from the earth, to focus on all that is heavenly.[10]

Elizabeth Johnson summarizes this trajectory and the feminist critique well, showing how it has sanctified hierarchical thinking, especially within the Christian tradition:

> Hierarchical dualism also shapes the classical Christian doctrine of God, who is depicted as the epitome of the masculine half of the dualistic equation. The all holy Other is uncontaminated by matter, utterly transcendent over the world and unaffected by it. The way in which patriarchal authority commands the obedience of women and other creatures on earth serves as a prime analogy for God's relation to the world.[11]

Johnson and other feminists have shown how this kind of thinking has permeated the practices of the Christian church throughout
the ages, engendering all kinds of oppression, leading finally to the
present ecological crisis. "Man alone bears the fullness of the image of
God," Johnson reminds us, "while women only deficiently so, and
nature not at all."[12] Overcoming this mind/body, spirit/matter, male/
female dualism has become a central project of feminist theology and
is crucial in any discussion of Holy Spirit, spirituality, or pneumatology
that claims a feminist perspective, including this one.

Interpreting Method

My entry into this conversation will be at first methodological. I
have already spoken of the genre or form of women's texts as contrib-
uting to their suppression. I have already noted that the very form of
theological texts, how well a text adhered to academic conventions,
has too often been the criterion for prestige or disparagement of that
text's author and her or his ideas. Doctrinal theology, most often taking the form of systematic genres, has taken precedence over spiritual
and even liturgical genres.[13] While adherence to formal conventions
is valued, all too often the form or shape of a text is ignored in the
work of interpretation; at best, form is viewed as a neutral container
for the content, which is assumed to be readily accessible to readers,
especially those trained in the prevailing rubrics and conventions.

A major claim of this study is that form matters. The genre or
form of a theological text, or of any text, for that matter, contributes
to the making of meaning in the interpretation of that text. Theological systems are shaped by the topics they address and by the very
ordering of those topics, an ordering usually based on a creedal format.
The message of a spiritual autobiography trades upon the narrative
structure created by its author, and upon the relative concreteness or
abstraction of the story it aims to tell. Prayers and hymns that arise
out of the practice of worship are powerful vessels of theological content precisely because of the artifice forged in their liturgical settings
and practice.

Form and content are no more separate than body and spirit,
mind and matter, heaven and earth. In fact, I am convinced that there
is a correlation, an analogy perhaps, a dynamic similarity between the
way form and content work together to create meaning in theological

texts and the way body and spirit are connected in the spiritual lives of human beings. Our bodies are temples of the Holy Spirit, even as Julian's *Showings* or Teresa's *Life* present to us the lived lives, the spiritual truth of their creators. As the rustic clay jars that preserved and protected the Qumran scrolls took value from and gave value to the treasure they contained, so earthen vessels have been the chosen dwelling place of God's Spirit, vessel and Spirit being mutually valued.

Embodying Theology

The central metaphor of this book is a metaphor of embodiment, and one that seeks to reflect upon and express the dynamic reality of an earthy, incarnate spirituality that, in turn, leads to constructive reflection upon the Holy Spirit. I have called the book *Sensing the Spirit*. While I certainly believe that embodied life is more than sensory experience, and though I certainly am not claiming that epistemological certitude is attached to sensory data, I find the fivefold imagery of human sense an apt form and structure for a consideration of Spirit and spirituality, for it grounds theological reflection in sensual imagery and in our somatic existence. The notion of "sensing" is key to this study in a number of senses.

The words *sensory* and *sensation* refer to how our five senses—sound, sight, taste, touch, smell—respond to stimulation from the outside world and from bodily existence. Our sensory organs are connected to our minds through the nervous system and interconnected with all the body's systems—respiratory, circulatory, skeletal, digestive. We often speak of the five senses as the way we take in information, reason as the way we process or interpret information. I am using the five senses as a hermeneutic scheme, a way of organizing the images I find in scripture, and those from the tradition that resonate with these biblical images. Does this model take in all possible images for Spirit? Probably not. But I think it goes a long way in reinterpreting, or making sense of, both biblical images and traditional pneumatology. By providing a somatic metaphorical structure, it also focuses the discussion of pneumatology in the created world and in bodily existence.

A second way of sensing has to do with the sense of a text: *sensus*, as in *sensus plenior* or *sensus literalis*, and with hermeneutics as *sense-making*, as making sense of texts within contexts. As Paul Ricoeur reminds us, we make sense, that is, we appropriate meaning, from our vantage point in front of the text.[14] The author's intent is inscribed in the text, and learning about the original context helps us in our sense-making; but we can never really inhabit the world of the author. The text itself has a sense, a world of its own, but interpretation takes place when we make sense of it for our own context, in what Hans-Georg Gadamer calls appropriation.[15] Sense-making is a dynamic process, not always readily apparent from the words on the page, but in a lively conversation with the text and its author from this side. This informs how I read scripture and historical texts and how I draw from the well of scripture for language and imagery that contribute to my constructive project. Genre or form works dynamically with what we call content in the work of interpretation.

At times I will also speak of sensing as *common sense*, or *phronesis*. We add a kind of practical wisdom to the information we receive from our sensory experience, a wisdom that is more than rationality.[16] We piece things together. For instance, when I'm flying and we hit a bump, I feel the motion and my hands start to sweat, I get a little dizzy, sometimes with a churning of the stomach or an increased heart rate. This is based not only on a kind of primal fear of flying, or on the mild sensation of turbulence, but on the knowledge and memory of plane crashes and the awareness that the plane is 35,000 feet up in the sky, seemingly defying the laws of nature. This information was taken in through the senses (reading the newspaper, watching television), but it also gets processed through human language and communication. Sense, reason, and practical experience work together. As a feminist, I will question the notion of reason as primal and speak instead of wisdom or intuition, which brings me to my final "sense."

I will also sometimes use the word *sensing* in a more intuitive, almost extrasensory way, a way we might call spiritual *sensitivity*. This explains why the scar on my back hurt when my sister had a melanoma years later in the same place. It explains why we often think about someone minutes before the phone rings, why we decide to stop and eat in one place rather than another and make a life-changing acquaintance, how we sense that someone is sad or upset or hurting, extrapolating beyond the subtle sensory signs. Folks as diverse as medical intuitives and faith healers describe experiences that suggest deep connections between body and spirit.[17] Even the medical profession is beginning to acknowledge the healing power of prayer. Just how do we learn to recognize the Spirit's groans when they are uttered?

Systemic Theology

I have said that form matters. I have given my project a form rooted in bodily existence by choosing the five senses as an organizing structure. While my scholarly identity is that of a systematic theologian, I am breaking the rules and conventions of that discipline in certain ways. I would prefer to call this a work of systemic theology, a term that I hope will be clear by the time we reach our conclusion. My methodology is hermeneutic and correlational, as are many respectable theological systems. I am certainly not alone or unique in my desire to ground theological reflection in bodily experience and biblical imagery. The doctrine of the Holy Spirit is the locus of this reflection and of my constructive project, but so is the realm of life in the Spirit called Christian spirituality. I will not rehearse the rubrics of Trinitarian theology or of theological anthropology in setting the stage for this pneumatological reflection. Nor will I begin with a survey of the "masters" on the subject, though my appreciation and critique of them will be evident throughout. My sources are largely in the spiritual mode, sometimes in the liturgical mode, and only occasionally in the doctrinal mode.

Systematic theology values order and logic; systemic theology values relationship and imagination. As the systems in our bodies are discrete yet interconnected, so the classic *loci* play into one another. Systematicians have argued about proper order; in systemic theology each of the classic topics becomes a hermeneutic key to the others and hence to the whole. Perhaps other topics should be added to the classics: sexuality, spirituality, imagination. It is my hope that this theology of the Spirit, which focuses first on the embodied life of the Spirit, will open out into a reinterpretation also of God's triunity, incarnation, revelation, creation, community, communion, and of our part as spirited, spiritual, inspired beings in the restoration and healing of all relationships.

I also hope that the *loci* themselves will continue to be redefined and renamed, as they have from time to time along the way. By starting with God-the-Father-Almighty, followed by Christ-His-only-Son-our-Lord, and finally by the Holy Ghost, theology's form and content, the relative values of its articles, are established in a pattern that resists creative thinking, imagination, and novelty—the very gifts the Spirit offers. The creeds that have given form and shape to doctrinal reflection provide an order and an agenda, but they also limit and exclude.

My own tradition is a confessional tradition, and I value the family history, the shaping of identity these texts provide. Fortunately, confessions and creeds are still being formulated, as ever, in the context of worship and dialogue. My hope is to keep the light and the breath and the lifeblood circulating, flowing, cleansing, renewing.

In honoring the body, I do not wish to glorify the body or to offer a reverse hierarchy in which matter, earth, and sensuality take precedence over mind, heaven, and spirit. The goal is integration, struggle, wholeness. Embodied life is both miraculous gift and painful limitation. Our senses take in the wonders of creation while we have them, but embodied spirituality must also promote the well-being of the blind and the lame, the brokenhearted and the prisoner, at least if it is to be a biblical spirituality. Lived life brings with it aches and pains as well as comfort and pleasure. And so life in the Spirit is always about comfort and affliction, encouragement and exhortation, warmth and cleansing, freedom and discipline.

I write from within a company of saints and sinners, in conversation with biblical characters, mystical visionaries, scholars, priests, and cantors. My conversations with feminists, reformers, and revolutionaries and with mystics and dogmatists will be overheard, I hope, in these pages. Rather than positioning myself in relation to these conversation partners at the outset, my perspective will emerge along the way. At times I dance around the margins of the church; at times I embrace orthodoxy; once in a while I venture away from home altogether. Rules are meant to be broken. The Spirit blows where she wills.

Spirit, Speech, Silence

Breath of Life

After hours of painful labor, of breathing deeply and quickly, a body comes from a body. Pain and hope, relief and anxiety spin together wildly as the tiny body, bloody, waxen, draws air into lungs and bellows. Tears of pain and joy flow together. The cord is cut; the child becomes a living, breathing soul. The grown-ups, who've been breathing on their own for many years now, are exhausted, delighted, relieved.

Inspiration, respiration, inhalation, exhalation, these are the evidence that a new life has begun. New birth is confirmed with a cry, the sound of air moving across vocal chords. Just so, embodied existence has begun for one of us, for all of us. The breath of life, the animating spirit, moves through the systems of bodies created in the image and likeness of God. New life breathes by the grace of God and depends on the grace of parents for sustenance and love.

Lungs, larynx, and lips give us the power to speak, to cry, to sing, to name, to praise, to pray. "I'll praise my Maker while I've breath," sang Isaac Watts.[1] "Let everything that breathes, praise the LORD,"sang the psalmist (150:6). The rush of God's Spirit, mighty and creative, blows also across wind pipes, forming words, language, speech. Finding a voice, speaking up, being heard into speech, these give our lives meaning and value, enabling us to make sense of things, including our lives as creatures related to God, to creation, to others, to self.[2] Just so, the sound of God's Spirit, the mighty wind of Pentecost, is the sound of human language, of being heard and understood, of preaching, proclamation, and praise, of song and speech and silence. For we do hear the Spirit in the "voices of peoples long-silenced,"[3] and in the quiet of contemplation and the listening ear.

Vocalizing is a physical activity, one we often think of as cerebral, but which engages our bodies from the neck down as well. Though even the best preachers often hide behind robe and pulpit, knees and wrists, diaphragm and shoulders take part in the work of proclamation.[4] Singers know they need to warm up, to stretch, to open their whole beings to the air that fills the chest and flows forth in song. In fact, all music, all speech, is so much wind, wind focused carefully by diction, pitch, and rhythm to convey a message, a message that struggles to make sense of things, to discern in the rush of air some truth.

The Spirit who gives us breath is the Spirit who makes a home in the temples of our bodies. A well-wrought sermon, a symphony, a sonata, has a certain form, a genre, a shape that aids preacher, musician, and hearer alike in grasping the message, in becoming involved in the creation of meaning that arises from any live interpretation of a text. Just so, theological reflection draws meaning from the form its author chooses. Form and content are partners in meaning-making, hardly separable; so God's Spirit forms a partnership with our bodies that enables us to live faithful lives within the possibilities and limitations of somatic existence.

In her novel *The Mind-Body Problem,* Rebecca Goldstein explores the philosophical, sexual, and spiritual dichotomies posed by bodily life.[5] Her hero is a Jewish woman, René (as in Descartes) Feuer, a beautiful but mediocre philosophy student who is married to an un-kempt mathematical genius. In her studies and her marriage, she is obsessed with resolving the tensions, bridging the gap between mind and matter. Knowing that in academe intellect matters above all else, René dares to voice her opinion, "Reality doesn't accommodate itself to the size and shape of the human mind." Her claim is discounted as "metaphysical" by fellow philosophers.

Goldstein's novel is but one of any number of books that have tried to grapple with the limits of language in speaking about physicality in relation to the life of the mind, the spirit, the soul, the psyche, the will, the emotions.[6] Even the words *inner* and *outer*, so often employed in spiritual writings, assume a valuation of the former at the expense of the latter. Rather than rehearse the conversations of the ages on the subject, which have resulted in perhaps too many words and too little consensus, I wish to borrow the Hebrew word *nephesh* to speak of the spiritual dimension of human existence, a dimension that complements *basar*, the fleshly dimension, and echoes *levav*, the heart. The hope is to find a way of speaking about mind and matter, heaven and earth, heart and soul, sense and spirit, that proclaims their integration and harmony and begins to overcome the dissonance and subordination that alienate us from the pleasures of creaturely life.

Hebrew Anthropology

Whereas English and Greek have many words to describe the more intangible aspects of human nature—spirit, soul, *pneuma*, will, emotions, *anima*, self, mind, *psyche*—the one Hebrew word *nephesh* encompasses a whole range of meaning. *Nephesh* evokes not only the "inner" dimension of human existence, but also the ideas of life itself, of living, breathing souls, of self and desire, of emotions and passion. Within the parallelism of Hebrew poetry, *nephesh* is often paired with *basar* (flesh) and *levav* (heart), terms that repeat and intensify one another. Perhaps reflection on these Hebrew terms can provide us with a way of speaking about spirituality that can begin to overcome the hierarchical dualism inherent in much Christian writing on the subject and can prepare the way for reflection on God's indwelling Spirit.

Nephesh, first of all, refers to life itself, to the breath of life, the animating power of creation. In Genesis, the breath of life is creative energy. God gave to all creatures the breath of life (*nephesh chayah*) (1:30) and by God's very own breath (*nephesh chayah*), *adamah* became living beings (*nephesh chayim*) (2:7). This breath of life connects human beings to God and gives them the power to name. The power to speak is often connected with this basic life force, as in Job:

> as long as my breath [*nephesh*] is in me
> and the spirit [*ruach*] of God is in my nostrils,
> my lips will not speak falsehood,
> and my tongue will not utter deceit. (27:3–4)

Another sense of *nephesh* is its reflexive usage, as in herself, himself, ourselves, yourselves. This evokes but is not altogether equivalent with the contemporary idea of "self" as developed in various psychotherapeutic theories.[7] Yet there is a sense of initiative, of agency, of autonomy, in the biblical notion of *nephesh* as self. For instance, Esther is urged to break silence by looking within herself, by questioning her own thinking: "Do not think [in yourself, your *nephesh*] that in the king's palace you will escape any more than all the other Jews. For if you keep silence at such a time as this, relief and deliverance will rise for the Jews from another quarter, but you and your father's family will perish. Who knows? Perhaps you have come to royal dignity for just such a time as this" (Esth. 4:13–14). A particularly striking example of this usage appears in Numbers 30, a statutory passage in which a woman's ability to speak "for herself" is subject always to the approval of husbands and fathers. The word *nephesh* in this reflexive sense appears some thirteen times in this passage. A woman's vows may stand only if her father or her husband remains silent; they are nullified if he speaks.[8] These and other passages suggest a deep connection between a person's basic being or selfhood and the power to speak freely.

Yet another sense views *nephesh* as the source of desire and appetite. All kinds of hunger and thirst arise from the human *nephesh*—a longing for God as well as lust and greed. The psalmist speaks often of a thirst for God, a longing that is associated with crying, singing, praying, praising: "God, my God, you I crave; my soul thirsts for you, my body aches for you…Your love is better than life, my speech is full of praise…I feast at a rich table, my lips sing of your glory" (63:1, 3, 5).[9] Closely connected with this sense is another, the idea that *nephesh* is the emotional center of human being. Like desire, emotion is expressed in words but flows from within. All emotions and passions, both love and loathing, distress and joy, originate in the *nephesh*. In joy and in sorrow the *nephesh* cries out to God: "Gladden the soul of your servant, for to you, O LORD, I lift up my soul" (Ps. 86:4). This sense has to do with crying out in anguish but also with listening to God's voice in the midst of struggle. The *nephesh* feels and hears and speaks God's passion and compassion.

Nephesh, in all its nuances of meaning, occurs throughout the literature of the Hebrew Bible, some 756 times, in poetry, prose, law, and wisdom. Its semantic richness enables us to draw together our thinking about human nature, to get behind the excesses of Greek and English semantics.[10] Though one Hebrew term can express many senses, a basic premise of Hebrew poetics is parallelism, which compares and contrasts, coupling linked terms to expand and intensify meaning. Our reflection on Hebrew anthropology can be enhanced, I think, by a brief consideration of two terms often used in parallel with *nephesh—levav* (heart) and *basar* (flesh). As Robert Alter has pointed out, parallelism is typical of Hebrew prose as well as poetry.[11] He focuses, as we will, on semantic parallelism, the use of two terms whose meanings are not altogether synonymous, to intensify or amplify meaning through poetic coupling.

The Hebrew terms *lev, levav* overlap semantically with *nephesh* and are often paired with *nephesh* to enhance its meaning.[12] Like *nephesh, levav*, which is usually translated "heart," can mean inner human being or self, appetite, desire, emotion, passion, but its semantic range also encompasses mind, will, and conscience. Heart and soul are used together throughout the Torah to describe a kind of completeness, the wholeheartedness with which God's law is to be obeyed: "You shall love the LORD your God with all your heart [*l'vevkah*], and with all your soul [*napheshkah*], and with all your might [*meodkah*]" (Deut. 6:5). The meanings of these terms are separate but overlapping, and their use together serves to amplify and intensify rather than separate and distinguish the meanings of each term.

The heart is a place of prayer and trust in God, the seat of praise: "Blessed be the Lord who hears my cry. God is the strong shield in whom my heart trusts. When help comes to me, joy fills my heart and I thank God in song" (Ps. 28:6–7, *The Psalter*). A heart that trusts God, a strong heart, is also linked with courage: "Be strong, and let your heart take courage, all you who wait for the LORD" (Ps. 31:24).[13] Heart is certainly seen as inner, inward, invisible, as the moral center of the human being: "The LORD does not see as mortals see; they look on the outward appearance, but the LORD looks on the heart" (1 Sam.

16:7). The human proclivity to see only the "outer" is being challenged; human wholeness includes both physical stature and spiritual center.

Both *nephesh* and *levav* are coupled at times with *basar* (flesh). *Basar* refers to humankind in general: "The glory of the LORD shall be revealed, and all people [*basar*] shall see it together" (Isa. 40:5). It speaks also of our kinship as male and female human beings: "This at last is bone of my bones and flesh of my flesh" (Gen. 2:23). Heart and flesh are distinct yet connected: "My flesh and my heart may fail, but God is the strength of my heart and my portion forever" (Ps. 73:26). By repeating and coupling these terms, human being is seen as an integrated whole: "My soul [*nephesh*] longs, indeed it faints, for the courts of the LORD; and my heart [*levav*] and my flesh [*basar*] sing for joy to the living God" (Ps. 84:2). Spiritual health and salvation are found in the completeness of human being: "Therefore my heart is glad, and my soul rejoices; my body also rests secure. For you do not give me [my *nephesh*] up to Sheol, or let your faithful one see the Pit" (Ps. 16:9–10).

This review of Hebrew anthropology has, I hope, helped us find a way of speaking about our spirituality as human beings who relate to God with heart, soul, and body. It seems clear that human/divine intercourse takes place within the wholeness and limitedness of creaturely existence, and that human language is the medium for divine/human discourse. We listen for God's windy words within and without; we cry out to God, ask God to give ear to our deepest longings; we utter thanks and sing praise with tongues fashioned by God's hand. Though human flesh is weak at times, frail and subject to pain and brokenness, enfleshed *naphshot* are created for relationship, and for communication with God's own Spirit.

Hebrew Pneumatology

It seems a curious irony that writers on Christian spirituality often make little mention of God's Spirit or of the spirituality of the Hebrew scriptures. Likewise, theologians wrestling with pneumatology emphasize the doctrine of the Holy Spirit in the church but reflect only in passing on the Hebrew Bible or the literature of Christian spirituality. Feminists have written much on spirituality but little on pneumatology. In this attempt to make sense of the biblical terms *spirit, soul, heart, body*, it is my hope that the deep connections between human and divine spirit, between our creation in God's image and God's creating Spirit, between our embodied existence and God's presence, can be reclaimed and affirmed. And this sense-making begins with the sense of sound, of hearing and speech, of wind and breath, of voice and silence.

We have begun with reflection on the language of human nature in the Hebrew Bible and have seen semantic connections between breath, life, speech, and passion. Human being is a wholeness, heart and soul, body and spirit, and mirrors the wholeness and holiness of God. *Ruach,* the feminine noun that means breath, wind, and spirit, speaks of human as well as divine life. Its semantic field overlaps in places with heart and soul; it encompasses both heaven and earth, and it is the word used to name God's Holy Spirit.

Ruach speaks of both divine and human breath. Job calls the speech of his consolers "windy words" (16:3). Idols have eyes and ears and mouths, but no senses, no ability to speak or breathe (Lam. 4:20; Jer. 10:14—51:17; Heb. 2:19; Ps. 135:17); the living God breathes and speaks. Word and breath are connected in creation: "By the word of the LORD the heavens were made, and all their host by the breath of [God's] mouth" (Ps. 33:6). God's breath can be creative or destructive. God's wind blows through the valley of the dry bones; *ruach* animates, revives, restores the life of Israel (Ezek. 37). God's wind blows away wicked chaff (Ps. 1) and rootless grass (Isa. 40).

All kinds of wind—the four winds, stormy winds, hot winds, rushing winds—are *ruach* from heaven. There is little distinction between weather and God's blowing. The wind of heaven caused the Red Sea to part (Ex. 15:8) and Noah's flood to subside (Gen. 8:1). A great wind blew as God "passed by" Elijah's cave (1 Kings 19:11–12), "but the LORD was not in the wind; and after the wind an earthquake, but the LORD was not in the earthquake; and after the earthquake a fire, but the LORD was not in the fire; and after the fire a sound [*qol*] of sheer silence [*dmamah dqah*]." God speaks to Elijah in a "still, small voice," a gentle whisper, a voice clear enough to be understood by human ears in the calm after the storm. This encounter with God serves to empower Elijah to get out of his despair, to take heart and obey. God, who commands the forces of nature, communicates with human beings (Ps. 107:25–29; Jer. 10:13; 51:16; Gen. 3:8–9).

Ruach evokes breath of life and windy words; it speaks of both human and divine spirit. As human spirit, *ruach* parallels both *nephesh* and *levav,* repeating yet expanding their meanings. It refers to animation, courage, disposition, and to the living, breathing being dwelling in *basar*.[14] Coupled with these parallels it evokes emotion, desire, mind, will, and moral character, but it also refers at times to a prophetic spirit, to a call from God to speak truth at the Spirit's urging. In this prophetic sense, spirit and speech go together: "And as for me, this is my covenant with them, says the LORD: my spirit that is upon you, and my words that I have put in your mouth, shall not depart out of your mouth, or out of the mouths of your children, or out of the mouths of your children's children, says the LORD, from now on and forever" (Isa. 59:21).

It is in this usage, as the power behind prophetic utterance, that *ruach* is identified with the Spirit of God in the Hebrew Bible. Clearly, *ruach elohim* was present in creation (Gen. 1:2), and the *ruach chai'im* dwells in all living creatures.[15] In the early days of Israel, the Spirit was seen as empowering its leaders, as in Judges.[16] From the time of Moses and throughout the historical books, God's Spirit is given to the leaders of God's people (Num. 11:17ff; 1 Sam. 10). In the prophetic books, the filling of God's Spirit, impelling truthful speech, is made explicit: "But as for me, I am filled with power, with the spirit of the LORD, and with justice and might, to declare to Jacob his transgression and to Israel his sin" (Mic. 3:8). Prophetic speech and action are inseparable:

> The spirit of the Lord GOD is upon me,
>   because the LORD has anointed me;
> …has sent me to bring good news to the oppressed,
>   to bind up the brokenhearted,
> to proclaim liberty to the captives,
>   and release to the prisoners;
> to proclaim the year of the LORD's favor. (Isa. 61:1–2)

Often the prophets speak for God in the first person: "I will pour out my spirit [*ruach*] on all flesh [*basar*]; your sons and your daughters shall prophesy" (Joel 2:28). Finally, God's Spirit becomes inescapable, ubiquitous: "Where can I go from your spirit? Or where can I flee from your presence?" (Ps. 139:7).

New Testament Spirituality

To claim that Hebrew thinking on human nature, spirituality, and God's Spirit is right and good and was cleanly supplanted by the corrupt Greek thought of the earliest Christian writers would be overly simplistic and dishonest. The language of *nephesh* and *basar* is as suggestive of dualism as *sarx* and *psyche*, or body and soul, and the Hebrew community was hardly devoid of patriarchy, as we have seen. A feminist hermeneutic will bring both suspicion and trust to the strands of tradition at hand, criticizing the androcentric bias of text and context but looking also for signs of hope, listening for the voices of spirited women. Hebrew poetics and language suggest a wholeness and an integration that have been distorted by traditional Christian readings. Yet the earliest Christian authors were Jewish, and the parallelism and wholeheartedness of Hebrew poetry is not entirely obscured in Christian scriptures. We know that the gospels and the writings of Paul have provided a seedbed for anti-Judaism as they have for hierarchical dualism.[17] Yet it is to these writings that we now turn, listening closely for some of that wholeheartedness and for a prophetic word.

The wind of the Spirit blows in the gospels and in the Acts of the Apostles. Here the Spirit's presence is linked with new birth and new life, with the wind of heaven, and with speaking, preaching, and witness-bearing. The spirit of prophecy, the voice of God, announces Jesus' ministry, through John the Baptist at the river Jordan and in the presence of Moses and Elijah on the Mount of Transfiguration. On both occasions a voice from heaven declares Jesus to be God's Son, God's chosen, God's beloved. At Jesus' baptism the Spirit appears "in bodily form, like a dove." At the transfiguration, the heavenly voice tells the disciples, "listen to him." Jesus the Jew is anointed prophet, and in the words of the evangelists, also Messiah, Lamb of God. God communicates with disciples and would-be disciples through the sound of human language; the Spirit who "spake by the prophets" speaks also in the teachings of Jesus.

The Gospel of John gives us two important narratives in which the Spirit blows and breathes. When the Pharisee Nicodemus comes to Jesus by night, Jesus teaches him about new birth in the Spirit—a spiritual birth like our physical birth. Nicodemus takes Jesus' words literally and is mystified. The mystery of this new birth is compared with the mystery of the wind: "The wind blows where it chooses, and you hear the sound of it, but you do not know where it comes from or where it goes. So it is with everyone who is born of the Spirit" (Jn. 3:8). Just as God breathed the breath of life into human beings at creation, just as God's Spirit animates each new life, so God's Spirit-breath gives Jesus' disciples their ministry of proclamation. After his disciples examined the bodily wounds of their risen Lord, Jesus breathed on them and said, "Receive the Holy Spirit" (Jn. 20:22). In this way he sent them into the world, giving them the ministry of forgiveness.

Perhaps nowhere are wind and words more closely linked than on the day of Pentecost, when those gathered heard "the sound of a mighty wind," and disciples began proclaiming the power of God in human language—utterance and understanding, both enabled by the Spirit (Acts 2:1–13). The work of the Spirit in the Acts of the Apostles is the work of proclamation and witness-bearing. God's redemption is communicated to Jews and Gentiles, to the nations, in human language and in the lives of faithful witnesses (*martyros*).[18]

Paul, who called himself a Hebrew of Hebrews, was also a Roman citizen, apostle to the Gentiles. Paul is an ambiguous figure for feminists, easy to discount. Women are to obey their husbands, to keep silent in church, to cover their heads. Yet Paul worked alongside women he named deacons and apostles; he proclaimed freedom from slavery and spiritual equality for male, female, Jew, and Greek. Paul speaks of *soma*, body, in positive spiritual terms but struggles against *sarx*, flesh. Our bodies are temples of the Holy Spirit (1 Cor. 6:19) and are to be presented to God as living sacrifice, holy and acceptable to God (Rom. 12:1). We have the treasure of God's reconciling gospel in earthen vessels, bodies both frail and invaluable (2 Cor. 4:7–11). Christ came to us in the flesh and, trusting us with the ministry of reconciliation, transforms us into the very body of Christ.

Yet Paul wrestled with *sarx*, that aspect of bodily existence that seems to work against spiritual health and well-being. In Romans 7, Paul tells of his conflict with *sarx:* "For I know that nothing good dwells within me, that is, in my flesh. I can will what is right, but I cannot do it" (18). *Sarx* does not equal *soma* for Paul (though the church has often confused them); it speaks of the limitations of somatic existence, of desire gone wrong. In Romans 8, Paul teaches about life in the Spirit, a passage crying out for dualistic interpretation but that also voices much wisdom. The Spirit of God dwells in us (9), gives life to our mortal bodies (11), bears witness with our spirit that we are children of God (16), groans with the labor pains of creation as we wait for the redemption of our bodies (22–23), and prays for us in sighs too deep for words (26). By God's Spirit, says

Paul, we confess our faith; by God's Spirit we are gifted for preaching, teaching, and prophecy (1 Cor. 12:4–11). By God's Spirit, we are urged to sing and pray and praise (Eph. 5:19; Col. 3:16).

Bearing Witness

The apostle Paul spoke also of scripture as God-breathed, as useful for teaching and for equipping the faithful (2 Tim. 3:16). This word "God-breathed" (*theopneustos*) appears only here in the New Testament and has been used by some to argue for the inerrancy of scripture. To say that "all scripture is God-breathed," in a personal letter that had not yet been canonized, begs the question as to what constitutes "scripture." The Greek term *graphe* does refer to sacred text, holy writ, and Paul would surely have considered the Hebrew Bible "*graphe*." Perhaps a more relevant question would be to ask what is meant by "God-breathed." If *ruach* and *pneuma* connote both breath and spirit, if human life is animated by this God-breath, then the inspiration that stirred the human speech of the biblical authors stirs faithful witnesses in all times and places.

As a theologian whose work is modified by a number of adjectives, including both "Reformed" and "feminist," I cannot go so far as to say that the texts and writings and speech of the faithful are sacred and holy in the same sense that the biblical witness is. Yet there is a sense in which the words of the faithful, both written and oral, are also God-breathed, inspired by the indwelling Spirit, prophetic in their witness-bearing, wise in their sense-making. Christian tradition can be seen as revelatory insofar as it is a continuation of the God-breathed conversation recorded in the pages of the Bible. Christian tradition is a gloss, a midrash on holy writ, forming a border, an expansion of the text like that of the sacred pages of medieval Jewish exegesis. The arguments and questions of the rabbis and teachers become a part of the interpretation of interpretation that is tradition.

But a Reformed approach is too trusting; feminist suspicion must also be raised. The problem with this model of God-breathed tradition is that women's words and wisdom are virtually excluded from the sacred pages of tradition. The beautiful sacred pages of women's recorded history are largely blank, snowy white from corner to corner as the "Blank Page" of Isak Dinesen's story.[19] Because tradition is largely written and because women have been excluded from the world of the literate until fairly recently, women's history has often been difficult to retrieve. When women did write, they did so in forms and genres deemed inferior and inconsequential. So the first step in interpreting tradition is to bring a critical eye to the androcentrism of history, learning about sexism first from the patriarchs themselves.

When this critical approach has made us angry enough, we are ready for the second step—beginning to interpret the silence, the absence of texts, the blank pages of women's history. We know women were there. We know that their stories have been erased or buried or ignored, told to others or taken to their graves. Pondering the blank pages, the lacunae, assuming erasure and effacement, feminist historians have begun to find new evidence: the mosaic of a bishop that once bore the name Theodora[20]; records of the Inquisition and the witch trials; a book by a beguine, long assumed to have a male author.[21] We continue to listen to the silence even as stories and voices emerge like so much invisible ink.

When we listen for women's voices in history, we hear them, and we begin to read and make sense of their texts until they begin to reform tradition itself, sometimes being received into the male-dominated "canon," sometimes forming a new body of literature altogether, "herstory." We realize that many women's texts have survived against great odds. We read these texts, like any texts, with both suspicion and trust, finding in them a new way of seeing and hearing the tradition, what Letty Russell and others call "a usable past."[22] The struggle to find a usable past, a history that embraces rather than alienates, is the constructive work of feminist hermeneutics and historiography, and it is both collective and personal, as Carol Lee Flinders points out: "At some point during the construction of a usable past, one finds herself drawing not merely on collective history or even imagined reconstruction of that history, but on personal history as well, and these bright bits of one's own remembered experiences as girlchild or woman complete the work."[23]

That women's voices are heard at all in scripture or tradition is evidence of the breath of the Spirit who inspires our speaking, who bears witness with us and within us. The apostle Paul urged women's silence, but he spoke also of the gifts of the Spirit and made no claim that these gifts are given on the basis of gender or social standing or any other criterion. Despite erasure and effacement, spirited women have exercised their spiritual gifts, have preached and prophesied, have confessed their faith and seen visions throughout the ages. This truth is the premise of an early collection of feminist traditioning, *Women of Spirit,* whose editors claim,

> It is characteristic of the leadership roles in Christianity claimed by women that they derive their authority from personal charism rather than from office…The Holy Spirit, unlike the institution, was recognized, even by the official tradition, as no respecter of persons.[24]

In my search for a usable past, I have been guided and heartened by those women who have continued to speak and write and listen to God's Spirit despite prohibition, and whose voices and texts attest to the ongoing presence of the Spirit. Their words come to us in strange ways at times, sometimes at the hands of editors and interpreters whose motives must be suspect even as we thank them for hearing and preserving these texts. It is a deep irony that the text of one of the earliest female witnesses, Vibia Perpetua, is included in the writings of Tertullian, who called women "the devil's gateway."[25]

The central core of this text is the autobiographical account of a young woman, Perpetua, who was put to death in Carthage in the early years of the third century.[26] A male catechumen, Saturus, continues the account, describing Perpetua's martyrdom and that of her friend, Felicitas. Tertullian has traditionally been considered the final editor, though more recent scholars are not so sure about this.[27] The persecutions of Septimus Severus were harsh, yet the faith of the North African Christians was fervent. Accounts such as this served to hearten the faithful, encouraging them to hold fast to their confession.

The account is an intriguing portrayal of the feminine, a mixture of androcentric and gynocentric perspectives. Perpetua, a woman of some wealth and social standing, has confessed her faith against great odds, for her witness separates her from her family, from her newborn child, and results in her death in the arena. Her father begs her to renounce her confession and she refuses:

> "Father," I said, "Do you see this vessel for instance lying here, waterpot or whatever it may be?"
>
> "I see it," he said.
>
> And I said to him, "Can it be called by any other name than what it is?"

And he answered, "No."

"So also I cannot call myself anything else than what I am, a Christian." (III)

The bodily reality of Perpetua's suffering is that of a young woman with babe at the breast; she considers it God's grace that her child was immediately weaned, that the milk in her breasts dissipated painlessly when she gave him to her father (VI). It is also God's will, according to Saturus, that her friend Felicitas gives birth while in prison, sparing the child the mother's martyrdom (XV). Saturus considers it the doing of the Holy Spirit, that the history is written (XVI). Perpetua also sees visions, some about milk and cows, but one in which she becomes a man, a young athlete ready for battle, fitting since the martyrs were viewed as spiritual athletes, but a shocking contrast to the young mothers' bodies that face the beasts. Though there is a kind of equality among the martyrs, saintly women throughout Christian history are required to transcend the limits of their gender in order to bear witness with their bodies.

The Rhetoric of Femininity

Perpetua's text bears elements typical of Christian women's texts throughout history. Its author is a woman who can write, compelled to record her experiences, and whose text survives, at least partly, because of male interests. The femininity portrayed is a special kind of femaleness—humble, fervent, transcendent. The author bears witness against great odds, believing herself to be empowered by the Spirit. Her witness is an embodied experience, essentially female, but a kind of masculinization is suggested. Like many spirited women, this early author received revelatory visions, described and inscribed in written words.

Elizabeth Petroff reminds us that there is a rhetoric of humility in most spiritual texts. Augustine, for instance, followed Cicero's advice, noting the expedience of an orator's "submissiveness and humility" in gaining the audience's ear. Such rhetoric is a way to set the stage for a human speaking on behalf of God, or in dialogue with God.[28] Yet women apologize also for their femaleness, men never for their maleness. Hildegard of Bingen, in a letter to Bernard of Clairvaux, seeks his advice about her visionary gift:

I am very preoccupied on account of a vision that appeared to me in the mystery of the spirit, a vision that I certainly did not see with the eyes of the flesh. I wretched creature, more than wretched, being a woman, since my childhood have seen great wonders which my tongue could not utter if the Spirit of God had not taught me, so that I should believe.[29]

Women are aware of their inferior status, yet they are compelled, nonetheless, to speak on God's behalf. Elisabeth of Schönau (1129–1165) opens her Second Book of *Visions* with this rhetorical approach. God's consolations, she says, are

not held in check by the muttering of those who think themselves great and disdain all that appears weaker…Because in these times the Lord deigns to show His mercy most gloriously in the weak sex, such men are offended and led into sin…While the men were given over to sluggishness, holy women were filled with the spirit of God, that they might prophesy, govern God's people forcefully, and indeed triumph gloriously over the foes of Israel.[30]

Petroff observes an orality in women's writing, lacking in the scholarly texts of men, even those of male mystics. She quotes Walter Ong, who notes that learned Latin "was sex-linked, a language written and spoken only by males, learned outside the home in a tribal setting which was in effect a male puberty rite, complete with physical punishment and other kinds of deliberately imposed hardships." [31]

Yet even unlettered women find their voices, with the encouragement of God's Spirit. So the rhetoric of humility is accompanied by the rhetoric of spirit-filled utterance. The Brother who copied and edited Mechtild's *Flowing Light of the Godhead* introduces it thus: "In the year of the Lord, AD 1250…this book was revealed in German by God to a Sister who was holy both in body and spirit." Mechtild's own voice soon speaks out, "Ah! Lord God! Who has written this book? I in my weakness have written it, because I dared not hide the gift that is in it."[32] Margery Kempe writes a whole "Proem" to her *Book* in the rhetoric of humility, describing herself as creature:

She knew and understood many secret things which would happen afterwards, by inspiration of the Holy Ghost. And

often, while she was kept with such holy speeches and conversation, she would so weep and sob that many men were
greatly astonished, for they little knew how at home our Lord
was in her soul. Nor could she herself ever tell of the grace
that she felt, it was so heavenly, so high above her reason and
her bodily wits; and her body so feeble at the time of the
presence of grace that she could never express it with her
words as she felt it in her soul.[33]

Dame Julian of Norwich also feels compelled to speak on behalf
of God despite her gender and her lack of education:

But God forbid that you should say or assume that I am a
teacher, for that is not and never was my intention; for I am
a woman, ignorant, weak and frail. But I know very well that
what I am saying I have received by the revelation of him
who is the sovereign teacher…But because I am a woman,
ought I therefore to believe that I should not tell you of the
goodness of God, when I saw at that same time that it is his
will that it be known?[34]

The words of these women are God-breathed; the Spirit of God
blows where she wills, and we hear the Spirit's sound in women's voices,
embodied, imperfect, concrete.

Of all the women mystics, perhaps Teresa of Avila is the best
example of the spirit-filled woman and the rhetoric of femininity.
Alison Weber offers us a powerful literary reading of Teresa's *obra*,
arguing that Teresa employed an intentional rhetorical strategy in order to be heard by multiple audiences, many of whom were hostile to
her message.[35] Erasmians and Lutherans, *conversos* and Jews,
alumbrados (illuminati) and those engaged in contemplative or "mental" prayer or who interpreted the Bible for themselves were all targets
of the Inquisition. Weber forcefully illustrates the urge of the Inquisition "to consolidate the power of a hierarchical mystery religion her-
metically controlled by priests." Their tactics included ensuring that
"sacred texts were inaccessible to the laity in general but to women in
particular, who were deemed to be mentally incapable of understanding the texts and inherently susceptible to diabolical influence." As
the daughter of a convert from Judaism, as one who practiced and
taught contemplative prayer, as an author and teacher who seemed to

have some familiarity with the Bible, and above all as a female, Teresa of Avila was suspect.

Teresa's writings may be read, her words may be heard as the rhetoric of a woman who wanted to be heard and understood within the context of misogyny. Weber argues, with good support, that Teresa is employing not just the rhetoric of humility, but other forms of rhetoric to win her hearers. Cicero's *captatio benevolentiae,* or conventional deference, is mixed with other persuasive strategies to gain the receptivity of her readers. Teresa is forced by the hostility of her context to write and teach, to offer a defense, to reform her order and the church skillfully, delicately, and with all the rhetorical subtlety she can muster. This is still a challenge for women who want to be heard within the contexts of patriarchy.

Teresa speaks as she writes, and her books are ostensibly about prayer, and in a variety of genres.[36] She models her *Vida* after Augustine's *Confessions,* a genre that stands between the narratives of the martyrs and the spiritual autobiographies of the mystics. The martyrs bear witness, Augustine bares his soul, but in the form of a prayer. Teresa's confessions, addressed to her confessors, are responses to charges of heresy, especially the practice of mental prayer. The whole notion of mental prayer, praying without moving one's lips, is an ironic twist on the silencing of women. Women are to be silent as Paul taught, but they must move their lips when they pray, presumably so the inquisitors can know what they're praying!

Teresa of Avila is a prime example of the double bind faced by spirited women then and now. She had to speak to defend herself against heresy, though teaching and writing were deemed heretical. Her *Vida* was at the request of her confessors, to quell the doubts of the inquisition. The *Way of Perfection* was written for the nuns but, as Weber points out, had to prove acceptable also to the *letrados.* The *Interior Castle* is a book of prayer, illegal yet required. Women are often deemed to be both heretics and heroes, dancing around the margins of the church, and yet remembered as prophetic. Teresa's books were burned by some, but she was made the first female doctor of the church after Vatican II. Faithful women must both transcend and abide by the limits of their gender to gain acceptance within the church; in doing so, they sometimes lose credibility with the radicals who dwell one step outside the church.

Just what criteria did the inquisitors use to determine whether Teresa's teaching was sound? What criteria do we use to determine whether such words are indeed God-breathed? Biblical prophets were critical of the status quo but took their authority from God's very Spirit. The Roman Catholic Church accepts "private" revelation as long as it is in keeping with traditional doctrine. Protestants use scripture as the test, yet we can see that those who hold the power to interpret also become guardians of the orthodoxy. These Spirit-filled women spoke from within the contexts of patriarchy, to offer both critique and support for tradition, both suspicion and trust, signs of a good prophet.

Perhaps a test of Spirit-breath is precisely this double bind, critique from both within and without the church, the dance of suspicion and trust, confession and protest.

In the *Interior Castle,* Teresa gives her sisters three ways to test the authenticity of God-breathed words. "There are many kinds of locutions given to the soul," she says. "Some seem to come from outside oneself; others, from deep within the interior part of the soul; others, from the superior part; and some are so exterior that they come through the sense of hearing, for it seems there is a spoken word."[37] She goes on to speak of three "signs" by which we can discern "whether or not they are from God." "The first and truest is the power and authority they bear, for locutions from God effect what they say" (120). The second sign is "the great quiet left in the soul, the devout and peaceful recollection, the readiness to engage in the praises of God" (121). Finally, true words "remain in the memory for a very long time, and some are never forgotten" (121). And so effective authority, quiet praise, and long memory become the tests of true prayer for Teresa, and the test of true speech for women of Spirit.

Women of Spirit

If Christian women who spoke and taught were often deemed heretics by the guardians of the orthodoxy, it makes sense that women often found a place to lead and preach in sectarian movements. The triumph of an orthodox tradition, if there is such a thing, is certainly no guarantee of its spiritual authenticity, for the history of the church is replete with the violent and repressive activities of those whose ideas held sway in the church. Not just the Spanish Inquisition and the Crusades, but the witch trials in Protestant lands and the oppression by Puritans of groups like the Quakers show the propensity for abuse of power throughout Christian history.

The Church of England originated as a reform of Roman Catholicism; the Puritans sought to reform Anglicanism. The Quakers arose in the wake of the English Civil War among those who were disillusioned with all kinds of institutional religion. George Fox wrote and taught of the Inner Light of God's Spirit and of the wisdom of God present in the lived faith of experience. This Inner Light could not be bound by class, social position, or gender, but was available to all, freeing any and all to speak. Despite loss of property, imprisonment, and death, faithful Quakers did speak out in an authentic and authoritative voice, and among them were many strong women.[38]

Among the Quaker women who bore witness with their lives and their voices was Margaret Fell, the widow who eventually became Fox's wife. Margaret preached and wrote and was repeatedly arrested for holding unauthorized meetings in her home. In her most famous tract, written while in prison, she uses biblical arguments to support the call of women to preach the gospel, noting the first witnesses to Christ's resurrection:

> Mark this, you that despise and oppose the Message of the Lord God that he sends by Women; what had become of the Redemption of the whole Body of Man-kind; if they had not believed the Message that the Lord Jesus sent by these Women, of and concerning his Resurrection? And if these Women had not thus, out of their tenderness and bowels of love, who had received Mercy, and Grace, and forgiveness of sins, and Virtue, and Healing from him; which many men also had received the like, if their hearts had not been so united and knit unto him in love, that they could not depart as the men did, but sat watching, and waiting, and weeping about the Sepulchre until the time of his Resurrection, and so were ready to carry the Message, as is manifested; else how should his Disciples have known, who were not there?[39]

If the Quakers were seen as a sect beyond Anglicanism or even Puritanism, the United Society of Believers in Christ's Second Appearing, the Shaking Quakers, or Shakers, were a sect beyond the Quakers. They, too, were led in the early days by strong female voices, especially that of Mother Ann Lee. Whereas the Friends were practiced at waiting in silence for the movement of the Spirit, the Shakers found the Spirit's movement to be somewhat less quiet, "often overflowing into emotion-charged manifestations—songs without words, strange languages, prayer through bodily gesture,...ecstatic spontaneous dancing, and disturbing bodily agitation and trembling."[40]

Soon after their British beginnings, the Shakers fled to North America in 1774. A visionary, Ann Lee was seen as "the Second Appearing of Christ in female form." The communities founded in America were committed to celibacy, to worship, and to work. While Shaker handiwork and their lively worship, which included dancing and singing, reflected the holiness of embodied life, their practice of celibacy is viewed with some suspicion by feminists. Marjorie Procter-Smith, in an important monograph, notes that though celibacy "freed women from the dangers of childbearing and gave them a measure of control over their own bodies...[C]elibacy was not unambiguously emancipatory for Shaker women."[41] Ann Lee's commitment to celibacy is shaped by the fact that she came into the movement from an unhappy marriage, having borne four infants, all of whom died; she often describes her spiritual life in images of labor, birth, and motherhood. Procter-Smith notes that though the movement became more patriarchal as it became more institutionalized, the egalitarian origins of the Shakers still have much to teach us about the freedom of the Spirit.[42]

The Shakers and the Quakers are but two of the many movements of the Spirit in which women's voices were raised despite the biblical mandate for silence. Martyrs and mystics, preachers and prophets have borne witness to God's presence in various families of faith, both inside and outside the mainstream of Christian tradition. They have played a prophetic role by bringing words of challenge as well as comfort to the faithful. Often these women were part of reforming trends, as in the Restoration movement of the early nineteenth-century American frontier. The women of spirit within the Restoration have become a special part of my own "usable past," as I have discovered both spiritual and familial ties with one particular branch, the Mulkeys of Kentucky.[43]

John and Philip Mulkey were Calvinist Baptists who began to question the doctrine of predestination, eventually leading their Kentucky congregations into the movement that the renegade Presbyterians Barton Stone and Alexander Campbell had begun, rejecting human creeds and seeking to restore the church to its New

Testament origins. One of the Mulkey daughters, Nancy, was a particularly powerful preacher— "a woman moved, and surely by the power of the Holy Ghost, to speak to the people," wrote Joseph Thomas in 1810, who was "astonished at her flow of speech and consistency of ideas."[44] Another eyewitness describes Nancy Mulkey's preaching:

> The youngest daughter in this remarkable family was a shouter, as then called…She would arise with zeal on her countenance and fire in her eyes, and with a pathos that showed the depth of her soul, and would pour forth an exhortation lasting from five to fifteen minutes, which neither father nor brother could equal, and which brought tears from every feeling eye.[45]

Hearing the stories of spirited women is empowering for those of us who today struggle to give voice to our deepest convictions in a church that does not always welcome our words, but when the woman is flesh and blood, the encouragement becomes palpable.

Hearing the Spirit

What have we learned about God the Spirit by listening to scripture and to the stories of those who have listened and borne witness to the Spirit's promptings? We have learned that the Spirit is free, blowing where she wills. The Spirit is not bound by gender, class, or geography, nor is she contained by the boundaries of the Church. God's Spirit speaks in the words of the faithful, but not only and always in the words of the orthodox. In fact, it would seem that the free-spirited Word of God often speaks in a tone of voice critical and suspicious of the dominant voices in the church. This liberated Spirit is also liberating, freeing the tongues of those long-silenced and filling the lungs of believers whoever and wherever they may be.

This freeing Spirit is also a birthing Spirit, a presence who animates the cries of new life, who endures the pangs of labor, and who offers the Church new beginnings and fresh perspectives. Reforming movements are often viewed as schismatic, divisive, yet if seen as fresh inbreakings of God's Spirit, as rushing wind blowing forth new understanding and utterance, the sound of Pentecost becomes a mighty chorus rather than babbling confusion.

True spirituality, embodied spirituality, may be described as wholeheartedness, as the integration of body and spirit, of *nephesh* and *basar*, of heart and soul. It is with this wholeheartedness that we hear and follow God's voice; it is wholeheartedly that we find the words to cry out to God, to sing praise, to speak a prophetic word, a comforting word, to tell our stories, and to make sense of all our relationships.

Wholehearted spirituality in the freedom of the Spirit gives us courage, courage to bear witness to God's grace against all odds, courage to speak despite efforts to silence us, courage to act authentically and in ways that encourage and empower the weak and the vulnerable. The Spirit gives us the wisdom to discern truthful moments, to bring both suspicion and trust to the interpretation of both past and present. As we listen to women of Spirit, we become women of Spirit.

Carol Lee Flinders has noted the tension between the feminist urge to find our voices and the spiritual, mystical urge to wait in silence. God's Spirit is heard in both silence and speech. We hear her in the gentle whisper, the still small voice in the center of our souls, and in the cries even of the voiceless. We hear her when we cry out to God in prayer, praise, and song, but also when we wait in quietness and longing. The *ruach* of God is mighty wind, stirring up Pentecostal tongues; the *ruach* of God is also the sound of sheer silence, a silence to be sensed and understood.

Vision, Verdure, Viridity

In the Garden

Digging in the garden, it makes perfect sense that life began in such a place, that we were created out of the mud of the earth, *adamah*, and that ultimately we belong in the garden. Some of my best theological thoughts come to me in the garden; spiritual knots are worked out in digging and weeding. Great mysteries occur to me: Why is it that the bugs and snails never eat the weeds but only the tender, temperamental plants, so carefully nurtured? Why is it that inedible walnuts fall from the neighbor's tree in bushels, but I can barely harvest a basket or two of strawberries before the birds get them? Compost is miraculous, clear evidence that new life comes from death and decay; worms are agents of creative transformation!

Springtime is a rebirth, especially in the northern climes. After months of frozen chill, of hard ground, leafless limbs, the first green shoots break through. In late fall and early winter I plant bulbs obsessively, a way of praying for spring to come. The first shoots usually appear around Ash Wednesday, that day when we see clearly our mortality, when we remember we are but dust and seek to find hope

31

in the sheer starkness of that reality. Through Lent spring takes hold, greening, growing. This drama, this dance, has become for me a primal image of the Spirit's life-giving creativity and energy— imperceptible, gradual, gentle power making way for sudden resurrection.

Miriam Therese Winter connects these words—humus, humor, human, humility—in a prayer:

> We humans share genetic qualities with humility, and laughter, and life.
> We have a lot in common with compost and the earth.
> We are destined to decompose like autumn leaves,
> like rotting fruit, we who are children of God and siblings of the stars.
> Reason enough to be humble when confronted by our own creativity,
> or when tempted to pretentious arrogance, reason enough to laugh.[1]

Perhaps hope can be imagined even on Ash Wednesday, if pastors and liturgists think of the rich, dark earth when we look into human eyes and say: "Remember you are but dust, and to dust you shall return." John Calvin is often remembered and discounted for his epithet that we are, we human, humus beings, but five-foot worms; one wonders whether Calvin realized how crucial those creatures are to the renewing of life. In Schiller's poem "Ode to Joy," set to music by Beethoven, even worms experience a kind of lustful ecstasy (*Wollust ward dem Wurm gegeben*). It is this earthy embodied creativity, shown forth in the greening processes of nature, that provides stimulation for the sense of sight as we reflect on the brooding, birthing Spirit of God.

The gardener knows she is a participant in ongoing creation, for in digging, weeding, planting, plucking, we encourage and enable life to flourish. The gardener cooperates with the forces of nature, with shadow and light, with sunshine and rain, with frost and humidity. When all is well in the garden, we get a glimpse of the rightness of things as they should be, of right relationships and the well-being of the whole. Times and seasons make sense; waiting and watching become crucial; temporality, transience, and fragility coexist peaceably with longevity and survival.

Theology has traditionally portrayed the Spirit as invisible, colorless, odorless, numinous, ghostly. Like Nicodemus or Elijah, we may hear the sound of it or even feel it passing by, but we gain nary a glimpse. Spirit seems by its very nature disembodied, amorphous, ethereal. Yet we believe in the Spirit's creative power; we call her "the Lord and giver of life." Perhaps, if we dig more deeply into the ground of scripture, we will see that the Spirit's creative presence is portrayed also in vivid visual imagery, the imagery of greenness, of verdure, of viridity.

Trinitarian theology has traditionally divided the labor among the three persons (Creator, Redeemer, Sustainer) or emphasized their internal relationships (Father, Son, Holy Ghost).[2] Yet there is also an insistence in tradition on the oneness of God, and of the Spirit's involvement in creating and redeeming as well as sustaining. Biblical faith teaches that the Spirit who brooded over the waters in creation is active in the ongoing work of creation and recreation. The sensual, somatic imagery of the Bible and of the created world suggests the unity of God who is Spirit and of her real presence in the living of life. In due course, more will be said about the Triune God; the systemic nature of this work will focus first on seeing things through the Spirit's eyes, and so this creating, greening, growth-giving power is seen to be the very Spirit of God, active in the world we inhabit.

Biblical Greenness

A whole cluster of Hebrew words speak of greenness and growth (*'arek / 'orek*), verdure (*chatzir*), green growth (*desheh*), luxuriant growth (*ra'an/ra'anan*), herbage (*'esev*), sprout (*tsmach/tsemech*). These words appear throughout the literature of the Hebrew Bible. Poetry and narrative use green images to describe creation and recreation, the sustenance of life, restoration, redemption, righteousness. Though these words are only rarely associated with *ruach*/spirit in an explicit way, the greening of the earth conveys God's presence and provision tangibly, visibly. Theological reflection upon this green imagery paints a picture of God's Spirit as a generative, growth-giving source of life and newness.

In creation, God caused the earth itself to spring forth with green shoots, grass, seed-plants, fruitful trees, herbage, verdure (Gen. 1:11–12; 2:8–9). Sprouting is both the activity and the product of this springing forth (Gen. 1:11–12). Green plants and fruit-bearing trees are given for food and for the well-being of all animals, including *adamah* (vv. 29–30). The fertility of these plants, their capacity for reproduction and regeneration, fits them for sustaining life and mirrors the fecundity of the whole created order. It was only as part of the curse that thorns and thistles were allowed to spring up (3:18).

In flood and plague, greenness was destroyed, but in each case new growth became a sign of recreation and restoration. Noah, a man of the soil (9:20), knew the flood was over only when the dove returned with a freshly-plucked olive branch. After the flood, both plants and animals are given for food; the grass, the green plants feed animals and humans alike. The first thing Noah did after the flood was plant a vineyard.

Plagues of hail and locusts destroyed all the greenness of Egypt (Ex. 9:22, 25; 10:12, 15; cf. Ps. 105:35). As slaves in Egypt, the Hebrews toiled to eke a living out of vegetable gardens; in the promised land, God will provide just the right climate and habitat for plants and grass, for milk and honey, for livestock and people to live securely (Deut. 11:8–17). This natural order of things, in which God provides for the people through a right relationship with the land, with one another, and with God has at its center the growing greenness of plant life and the cycles of nature.

In the poetic and prophetic writings, greenness becomes a sign for God's blessing and care, for the well-being of life, for right relationship with land and the created order, for spiritual health and wholeness. Dryness, rootlessness, withered leaves, and fruitless branches are signs of faithlessness, exile, and despair.

Green imagery occurs throughout the Psalms and teaches of God's provision and creative presence, which become an occasion for praise.[3] "You tend and water the land. How wonderful the harvest! You fill your springs, ready the seeds, prepare the grain. You soak the furrows and level the ridges. With softening rain you bless the land with growth" (Ps. 65:10–11). Psalm 104, another song of praise and delight in creation, views the created order as evidence of God's care and nurture: "Birds nest nearby and sing among the leaves...You nourish the earth with what you create. You make grass grow for cattle, make plants grow for people, food to eat from the earth" (104:12–14). The creativity of God is embodied in the created world: "God, how fertile your genius! You shape each thing, you fill the world with what you do" (104:24). God's praise is sung in Psalm 147, again with strong visual imagery: "The Lord stretches the clouds, sending rain to the earth, clothing mountains with green" (147:8).

Verdant images teach also of the Spirit's renewing and refreshing life: "You give me rest in green meadows, setting me near calm waters, where you revive my spirit" (23:2). Spiritual health and growth are likened to healthy, well-rooted trees: "You will stand like a tree, planted by a stream, bearing fruit in season, its leaves never fading, its yield always plenty" (1:3; cf. Jer. 17:8). A healthy relationship with God is evidenced by long life, prayer, and continued vitality: "The just grow tall like palm trees, majestic like cedars of Lebanon. They are planted in the temple courts and flourish in God's house, green and heavy with fruit even in old age" (Ps. 92:12–14).

Greenness is a sign of faithfulness, both human and divine: "But I am like an olive tree growing in the temple court, I trust God's love for ever" (52:8). Blessing is likened to fertility: "May wheat be thick in the fields, fruit trees sway on the slope. May cities teem with people, thick as the forests of Lebanon" (72:16). In this healthy, spiritual realm, right relationship extends to all: "Fidelity sprouts from the earth, justice leans down from heaven. The Lord pours out riches, our land springs to life" (85:11).

Yet, in the parallelism of Hebrew poetics, these same images can be used to show comparison and contrast. If the righteous are like deeply rooted trees, the wicked are like chaff blown away by the wind (1:4). Sinners do not survive in the Spirit's realm but "wither like grass, they wilt like young plants" (37:2). The wicked flourish at first, then vanish (37:35–36). Human faithlessness is contrasted with God's faithfulness: "Scoundrels spring up like grass, flourish and quickly wither. You, Lord, stand firm for ever" (92:7–8).

Even as the vitality of greenness represents spiritual health and well-being, the transience of green things becomes a poetic image for the fragility of life. Psalm 90, the basis of Isaac Watts's hymn "O God Our Help," speaks of this temporality: "You sweep away the years as sleep passes at dawn, like grass that springs up in the day and is withered by evening" (90:5–6). Despair and disorientation are also part of the fragility of life: "My heart withers away like grass. I even forget to eat…My days pass into evening, I wither like the grass" (102:4, 1).

The psalmist hopes that the enemy will prove weak as well: "Let those who hate Zion be ashamed and retreat! Let the east wind dry them up like weeds on a rooftop" (129:5–6).

The parallelism between permanence and temporality, between rootedness and exile, is a favorite also of the prophets, who employ this green imagery to speak of exile and restoration and of the surprising and imperceptible process of redemption. In Isaiah, for instance, verdant imagery is employed to describe the experiences of unsettledness and of hope, of exile, and of return.[4] Right relation with God and the land are associated with healthy growth in all three sections of the prophecy, enemies with blight. A pivotal passage opens Second Isaiah:

> A voice says, "Cry out!"
>   And I said, "What shall I cry?"
> All people are grass,
>   their constancy is like the flower of the field.
> The grass withers, the flower fades,
>   when the breath [*ruach*] of the LORD blows upon it;
>   surely the people are grass.
> The grass withers, the flower fades;
>   but the word of our God will stand forever. (40:6–8)

This familiar passage seems to challenge the verdant imagery of good growth and right relationship laid out thus far. The transience of life, including human life, is contrasted with the powerful breath of God and the permanence of God's word. Yet these words seek to comfort the exiles in their final days of captivity. Subsequent chapters paint a hopeful picture of the new creation, of the new things that will spring forth (42:9). The promise of God's blessing is offered to the captives: "For I will pour water on the thirsty land, and streams on the dry ground; I will pour my spirit upon your descendants, and my blessing on your offspring. They shall spring up like a green tamarisk, like willows by flowing streams" (44:3–4). Cyrus is named as the deliverer; restoration is in sight: "Shower, O heavens, from above, and let the skies rain down righteousness; let the earth open, that salvation may spring up, and let it cause righteousness to sprout up also; I the LORD have created it" (45:8).

The Spirit's power in creation and recreation is shown once again in the promise of restoration and return. God's word is of the utmost comfort to the homeless, rootless exiles. Rather than placing the eternal word over and against the temporality of creation, God's word is seen as surpassing even the glory of creation, as providing the very creative power that enlivens creation:

> For as the rain and the snow come down from heaven,
>   and do not return there until they have watered the earth,
> making it bring forth and sprout,
>   giving seed to the sower and bread to the eater,
> so shall my word be that goes out from my mouth;
>   it shall not return to me empty,
> but it shall accomplish that which I purpose,
>   and succeed in the thing for which I sent it. (55:10–11)

Restoration, the restoration of right relations, of righteousness, is announced by the prophet in language of healing and salvation, again linked with verdant images. Isaiah 58 speaks of the healing that shall "spring up quickly" (v. 8); the righteous shall be "like a watered garden" (v. 11). Right relationship is restored as the homeless return home: "For as the earth brings forth its shoots, and as a garden causes what is sown in it to spring up, so the Lord GOD will cause righteousness and praise to spring up before all the nations" (61:11).

Creation, recreation, exodus, and restoration are all the work of God's Spirit, the Creator's enlivening presence in the lived lives of breathing, sensual human beings. This work of redemption is given yet another greening image in the language of the prophets—the righteous branch, the redemptive shoot from the stump of Jesse.

> A shoot shall come out from the stump of Jesse,
>   and a branch shall grow out of his roots.
> The spirit of the Lord shall rest on him,
>   the spirit of wisdom and understanding,
>   the spirit of counsel and might,
>   the spirit of knowledge and the fear of the LORD. (Isa. 11:1–2)

Not just Isaiah, but Jeremiah, Ezekiel, and Zechariah speak of a Branch, the horn of salvation, that will spring up, bringing justice and righteousness. While Christians see in these prophecies a sign of the Incarnation, the Hebrew people find in them hope for a wise and just rule. In righteous branch or verdant pastures, the Spirit's redeeming and restoring activity is made visible.

Gospel Gardens

The parallelism of Hebrew poetry reflects a way of thinking carried into the Christian scriptures but often given a dualistic interpretation. We have seen that the imagery of greenness and viridity is used in varying ways, not uniformly positive or negative. Hebrew poetry is able to portray the powers of death and life, of righteousness and wickedness, of permanence and transience in the same breath. The Spirit's work is both greening growth and withering judgment, both comfort and affliction, both planting and plucking.

In the gospels, Jesus' teachings are replete with agrarian and organic imagery. The providential care of God is evidenced in the splendor of field and flower, as is the temporality of bodily existence (Mt. 6:28–30; Lk. 12:27–28). Jesus repeatedly uses imagery of healthy fruitful trees to represent human faithfulness, and fruitless trees, falsehood (Mt. 7:15–20; 12:33; Lk. 6:43–45). The fig tree becomes a sign of the times (Mt. 24:32–33; Mk. 13:28–29; Lk. 21:29–31), a sign of warning to the faithless (Mt. 21:18–22; Mk. 11:12–14, 20–26), and a sign of God's patient grace (Lk. 13:6–9). While dualistic readings have taken these teachings of Jesus to be favoring spirit over body, mind over matter, and privileging certain groups of believers, a more Hebraic reading sees lily and fig tree as indicative of the transcendence and the transience of all embodied life.

Jesus' parables, of fig tree, leaven, and mustard seed, of vineyards, harvests, and weeds, use familiar natural imagery to teach about the divine/human relationship, the life of the Spirit. Jesus' teachings are multivalent and bear repetition; they never neatly divide the good from the bad; they address all kinds of hearers, with all kinds of faith. The parable of the sower (Mt. 13:1–9,18–23; Mk. 4:1–9,13–20; Lk. 8:4–8,11–15) may well be read as a kind of midrash on the prophets and psalms. Any hearer would want to identify with the good and healthy soil, in which God's word takes root and yields abundantly, but all hearers will, at times, identify with the well-worn path, the rocky ground, and the thorny patches.

The tensive multivalence of the green images in Jesus' teachings is evident also in the gospel of John, where Jesus describes himself as the true vine, his father as the vinedresser, and the disciples as the branches (Jn. 15:1–11). The central message, that the disciples are to abide in Jesus and Jesus in them, teaches about the relationship between

God, Christ, Spirit, and disciple. Fruitfulness is the goal; pruning and trimming are inevitable. Once again, the health and well-being of life in the Spirit depend on new growth as well as radical discipline. One wonders whether Paul knew of this teaching of Jesus. He struggled to make sense of Jewish-Christian relations, using imagery of root and branches, of in-grafting and off-cutting; he speaks of both the kindness and the severity of God (Rom. 11:16–24). Paul saw the nurture of new disciples as a cooperative effort, like gardening (1 Cor. 3:6–9). He certainly spoke of spiritual maturity in terms of fruitfulness, and in a way that has given rise to dualism, as we have seen, contrasting the fruits of the flesh (*sarx*) with the fruits of the Spirit (Gal. 5:16–26). If spirit is seen as that which overcomes, or subdues bodily passions, and if all bodily desires are seen as evil, then a theology of embodied spirituality seems a contradiction in terms. Yet, here as elsewhere, we see that Paul is not equating *sarx* and *soma*, nor is he denigrating the body. I believe it is a dualistic reading of these texts that has confused the issue in Western Christian theology, and though some of this dualism may be part of the author's intent, this is not the only way to make sense of his words. Again, the parallelism of Hebraic thought, which embraces the varied values of lived life, can read Paul's teachings on spiritual fruitfulness in a way that builds on the poetry of the Psalms and prophets and on the parabolic teachings of Jesus.

The witness of scripture begins and ends in the garden, of creation and new creation; the tree of life grows in both (Gen. 2:8–9; Rev. 22:1–2). This tree, like that of the Psalms and of Jeremiah, is well-rooted, well-watered, and fruitful. The tree of life in Revelation's heavenly city portrays the qualities of spiritual health and well-being taught by the green imagery throughout scripture. Creation, recreation, renewal, and righteousness are visible. So are redemption and reconciliation, for this tree's green leaves are "for the healing of the nations" (v. 2).

Verdant Spirituality

As we consider the sense of sight and the ways that the Spirit of God is known through verdant visual images, it seems only right that we turn to the spiritual writings of two women whose visions formed the basis for their theological reflection. Faithful people in varied times and places have told of special revelations from God in the form of visions. The Middle Ages were a time when visionary literature abounded in the Christian world and elsewhere. The genres of spiritual and mystical writing were employed by monks and nuns, scholars and laypeople to convey religious experience, particularly direct encounters with God. This literature is one of the few places where women's texts have been preserved and in which their voices are heard firsthand.

Two of the most well-known women mystics, Hildegard of Bingen (1098–1179) and Julian of Norwich (1342–1423?), recount their visions of divine encounter in texts that have been preserved and translated. While their historical contexts differ, as does their literary output, both take great care in describing the details of these visions and in putting forth their spiritual insight. Hildegard was a Benedictine abbess who lived a fairly public life and corresponded with priests and popes. Julian lived a reclusive life, wrote one book in two versions, and left only the scantiest biographical details. Yet both women were moved to put their thoughts into writing, and both employ vivid visual imagery, including the green imagery of spiritual growth.

Hildegard's first major text, *Scivias*, is an extended theological work. In the third section, as she teaches of the virtues and the spiritual gifts necessary for their generation, she employs a number of images, including organic language. She speaks of the virtues as fruit in Book Three, Vision Three. Here she also speaks of the four elements—fire, air, water, and earth—and of the five senses.[5] In subsequent visions, she develops her trinitarian theology and begins to speak of the Savior in organic terms, with many biblical references. Jesus plants fruitfulness and power in the good trees, the souls of the virtuous (432–3). He is the flower emerging from the branch of the root of Jesse (436–9). The triune God is bound together with the faithful by means of this virtuous power: "The Spirit of the Lord is known by the strong virtues that shine forth from It, as branches grow from a root; so there is one God from Whom all good things come and through Whom all things are wisely disposed" (438). In Vision Ten such imagery is expanded in the analogy of the field (474–9), reminiscent of Jesus' parables: "To a person who willingly and with a good heart receives the seed of my word, I grant the gifts of the Holy Spirit in superabundance, as to a good field" (475). The final vision, "The Symphony of the Blessed," is a sequence of heavenly songs, containing images of green branch, flower, stem, and root: "O noble verdure, which grows from the Sun of splendor!" (528).

Hildegard here is beginning to see verdure as the spiritual power that produces virtue in the lives of believers. This idea is developed more fully in a later work, *The Book of the Rewards of Life*.[6] In these visions a man, God, turns to the points of the compass and teaches about spiritual virtues and holiness. In the Fourth Part, God is seen as standing "up to the calves of his legs in moisture and greenness and is sprouting because the earth contains what God has bound together" (185). The virtues are seen as the outgrowth of this rootedness in God and the creation.

> For the soul in which God is, as in the earth, from the begin-
> ning of its strength to the perfection of good and holy works,
> as it were, from his knees right up to the calves of his legs,
> contains the sighs, prayers and holy works that lead to God,
> just as the moisture, greenness and the sprouts of the earth
> contain the grace of God. (186)

Here is Hildegard's notion of *viriditas* given full flower, so to speak. The fertile soul sprouts virtue and strength. Spiritual power is made available through the element of earth.[7]

The anchoress, Julian of Norwich, wrote one book, *Showings*, in two versions.[8] The Short Text was written soon after her visions took place, when she was "thirty and a half years old." The Long Text is a careful expansion of the Short and was written some twenty years later. We have very few historical details about Julian's life. We know that she became an anchoress following these visions and spent her life in a cell attached to the church for which she is named. Her cell had two windows: Through one she partook of worship; through the other she offered spiritual counsel to visitors.

The *Ancrene Riwle*, by which Julian lived, allowed for a garden, a cow, and a cat.[9] The notion of Julian as a gardener is appealing, though she likely had a servant of some kind who provided for her daily needs. The lacunae in biographical details allow for imaginative reading of Julian's concrete language. The central parable of the Long Text tells of a servant, a gardener who digs for treasure in the earth:

> I watched, wondering what kind of labour it could be that
> the servant was to do. And then I understood that he was to

do the greatest labour and the hardest work there is. He was to be a gardener, digging and ditching and sweating and turning the soil over and over, and to dig deep down, and to water the plants at the proper time. And he was to persevere in his work, and make sweet streams to run, and fine and plenteous fruit to grow, which he was to bring before the lord and serve him with to his liking. (273-4)

The interpretation of this parable, which is primarily christological, makes up one third of the Long Text. Julian interprets the parable in exacting detail, having contemplated it for some twenty years. The servant is both Christ and Adam (274). Julian's trinitarian theology is reminiscent of Augustine's, for she speaks of the Holy Spirit as the Love between the first two persons: "The lord is God the Father, the servant is the Son, Jesus Christ, the Holy Spirit is the equal love which is in them both" (274).[10] The servant, Jesus, descended into hell and "raised up the great root out of the deep depth, which rightly was joined to him in heaven"[11] (277).

Julian is careful to keep the three persons closely bound at all times. She is aware of the paradox and ambiguity of christology, of the Trinity, and of the spiritual life: "During our lifetime here we have in us a marvelous mixture of both well-being and woe *(wele and woo)*" (279). Her words bring comfort and theological insight: "Before he made us he loved us, and when we were made we loved him; and this is made only of the natural substantial goodness of the Holy Spirit" (283). For Julian, as for Hildegard and the Hebrew poets, God's Spirit is present to us in all the vicissitudes of earthly life, connecting us with creation and neighbor.

Celtic Spirituality

Even as the writings of the mystics are being rediscovered in our day as an unmined lode in Christian tradition, so the worship, theology, and art of Celtic Christians are providing a new wealth of insight. Collections of Celtic prayers and stories abound.[12] Scholars of Celtic Christianity are struck by the earthiness of its poetry, prayers, and stories. Oliver Davies and Fiona Bowie see a link between the physicality of Celtic asceticism and "a persistent emphasis in the Celtic texts upon the place of nature within the Christian revelation."[13] In both the medieval texts and the oral traditions more recently collected, the reader is struck by vivid imagery from nature—plant, animal, and mineral—as this sixth-century Irish litany illustrates:

O star-like sun,
O guiding light,
O home of the planets,
O fiery-minded and marvelous one,
O fertile, undulating, fiery sea,
Forgive.[14]

The Gaelic poems and prayers collected in the nineteenth century by Alexander Carmichael are rich evidence of this Celtic emphasis on life embodied in the natural world.[15] The *Carmina Gadelica* contains prayers and blessings for everything from milking to firebuilding and washing, to eating, sleeping, and healing. Blessings for animals, birds, and livestock abound; an entire collection offers thanks for plants like silverweed, club-moss, ragwort, and bog myrtle and invokes their healing and protective powers.

Thou ragwort! thou ragwort!
And thou woman who plied the ragwort!
If the dead of the grave should rise,
The plying of the ragwort would be remembered. (367)

While some of these incantations seem superstitious and magical to our modern minds, the Celts saw in these plants a reason and a reminder to pray to the divine powers that created them, and a way of renewing their faith and spiritual health:

I will call the pearlwort
Beneath the fair sun of Sunday,
Beneath the gentle hand of the Virgin,
She who will defend me,
In the might of the Trinity
Who granted it to grow.

While I shall keep the pearlwort,
Without wile shall be my lips,
Without guile shall be mine eye,
Without hurt shall be mine hand,
Without pain shall be mine heart,
Without heaviness shall be my death. (370)

These Celtic Christians saw all of creation as infused with the imaginative, life-giving, healing energy of God, and they saw their own bodies as part of a world animated by the Spirit, yet utterly dependent on the Three, the Triune of grace.

Natural Theology

The sixteenth century was a time of all kinds of sea changes, including a turning of the tides, a revolution of sorts in the sense of sight. Explorers and artists alike began looking and seeing, observing the world in new ways, and with new tools and instruments. Ground lenses and polished mirrors enabled the invention of microscopes and telescopes; Renaissance men and women could now view heaven and earth in a new light, bringing into focus worlds previously unseen.

The visual art of Albrecht Dürer reveals well this new way of seeing. Many of Dürer's paintings portray traditional religious subject matter; his etchings often reflect Reformation ferment. It is his paintings and drawings of subjects from nature—a hare, the feathered wing of a bird, a clump of grass—that revolutionize visual art, for these natural representations not only find their way into his "sacred" art, they represent creation itself as artistic and sacred.[16]

Born a generation after Dürer, yet often viewed as an iconoclast, John Calvin had a keen sense of sight and a penchant for the visual. Invoking Calvin's name in the midst of all this reflection on nature and vision begs the question concerning the place of natural theology. Is all of this green imagery not a reading into scripture a kind of ecofeminist Romanticism? Can a theologian who sees herself as both feminist and Reformed skirt questions about analogy, special revelation, and the priority of the Bible? By no means. In fact, I believe that it is precisely Calvin's teaching concerning revelation and natural theology that gives force to the approach I have taken and provides a key to pneumatology as well.

Calvin uses vivid visual language even as he views visual images for God as idolatrous. "Surely," he says, "there is nothing less fitting than to wish to reduce God, who is immeasurable and incomprehensible, to a five-foot measure."[17] A word, for Calvin, is worth a thousand pictures. Painting and sculpture are gifts of God but must portray "only those things…which the eyes are capable of seeing" (I.xi.12).

But if visual images are unacceptable, verbal images are fine. In his first book, *Knowledge of God the Creator*, Calvin paints striking pictures of the created order, drawing heavily from the biblical ground we have sampled. Nature does teach us something of God:

> There are innumerable evidences both in heaven and on earth that declare his wonderful wisdom...which thrust themselves upon the sight of even the most untutored and ignorant persons, so that they cannot open their eyes without being compelled to witness them. (I.v.2)

Calvin, while shunning idolatry, is particularly fond of optical metaphors. The human eye cannot see God, yet the created order (I.v.1), humankind (I.v.3), the works of God (I.v.11), and the words of Moses (I.viii.7) are all likened to mirrors that reflect the image of God. Mirrors and lenses make the invisible visible. Here Calvin employs a striking optical metaphor to illustrate the relationship between natural and biblical revelation:

> Just as old or bleary-eyed men and those with weak vision, if you thrust before them a most beautiful volume, even if they recognize it to be some sort of writing, yet can scarcely construe two words, but with the aid of spectacles will begin to read distinctly, so Scripture, gathering up the otherwise confused knowledge of God in our minds, having dispersed our dullness, clearly shows us the true God. (I.vi.1)

We make sense of the natural world, we see God in it and behind it, through the lens of scripture. Knowledge of God is not limited to the words on the pages of the Bible, yet these pages help us make sense of everything else, including our creaturely existence. Reflection on the book of nature is through the lens of biblical faith.

Just as scripture is a sense making spectacle for embodied spirituality, focusing the relationship between creature and creation, so also the indwelling Spirit clarifies the relationship between creature and Creator: "The testimony of the Spirit is more excellent than all reason. For as God alone is a fit witness of himself in his Word, so also the Word will not find acceptance in [human] hearts before it is sealed by the inward testimony of the Holy Spirit" (I.vii.4). The Spirit who broods over creation, who spake by the prophets, makes a home in human heart, mind, soul, and strength, bringing all things into focus.

Romantic Hermeneutics

The charge of Romantic ecofeminism is one I will gladly accept, if I can further define these terms. The Romantics—poet, painter, and philosopher alike—sought organic connection with the natural world, seeking a kind of spiritual wholeness, and this in reaction to the reasoned approach of the Enlightenment. Peter Gay, in his classic portrayal, speaks of the *philosophes* as rejecting the enchanted universe of ages gone by.[18] The Romantic Movement was, in a sense, a re-enchantment following the dis-enchantment of the Age of Reason.

Not all Romantics viewed the natural world through rose-colored glasses. In fact, the Romantic poets often had a healthy respect for the violent and malevolent power of nature. It was, after all, Tennyson who wrote,

> Who trusted God was love indeed
> And love Creation's final law—
> Though Nature, red in tooth and claw
> With ravine, shrieked against his creed—[19]

The urge to interpret the book of nature, to nurture a connection between human and divine imagination, inspired much Romantic poetry. The created world was seen as a superior source of truth and wisdom, as these lines from Wordsworth suggest:

> Books! 'tis a dull and endless strife;
> Come, hear the woodland linnet,
> How sweet his music! on my life,
> There's more of wisdom in it…

> One impulse from a vernal wood
> May teach you more of man,
> Of moral evil and of good,
> Than all the sages can.[20]

Wordsworth's friend Samuel Taylor Coleridge, poet, philosopher, and theologian, provides further insight into the relationship between Creator, creation, and creature. For Coleridge, the power of imagination provides the connection. "The primary IMAGINATION I hold to be the living power and prime Agent of all human Perception, and as a repetition in the finite mind of the eternal act of creation in the infinite I AM."[21] Imagination, for Coleridge, is a divinely given power, a partner with reason, supersensory.

Coleridge is perhaps best remembered as a poet and literary critic, but his theological contribution has gained renewed attention in the last decades. *Confessions of an Inquiring Spirit*, published in 1840, six years after Coleridge's death, presents his thoughts on biblical interpretation.[22] The unifying power of imagination is given a concrete instance in the reading of scripture, a reading oddly reminiscent of Calvin's:

> I have said that in the Bible there is more that *finds* me than I have experienced in all other books put together; that the words of the Bible find me at greater depths of my being; and that whatever finds me brings with it an irresistable evidence of its having proceeded from the Holy Spirit. (43)

Like Calvin, Coleridge recognizes human fallibility, a recognition not usually associated with Romanticism: "What the right interpretation is,—or whether the very words now extant are corrupt or genuine—must be determined by the industry and understanding of fallible, and alas! more or less prejudiced theologians" (61).[23]

A Romantic such as Coleridge can help us interpret both the book of nature and the book of scripture in ways that affirm the presence of God's Spirit in the process. Imagination is seen as the very creative power of God, the energy that animates creation and that gives the faithful poet or theologian ways of speaking, word pictures appealing to spirited vision. Both books present us with the full spectrum of visual truth—the interplay of finitude and ultimacy, life and death, time and eternity; the one helps make sense of the other.

Contemporary Observations

This foray through the natural world by way of scripture, the mystics, Calvin, and the Romantics may seem at once circuitous and familiar. Mine may seem an odd mapping of the terrain, a disorienting vista. To be sure, much of this ground has been covered by others in more systematic and orderly outings. By way of conclusion, conversations with some of those others are certainly in order.

Creation Spirituality

These observations of the Spirit's presence in the created world are clearly creation-centered but diverge from creation spirituality in important ways. Barbara Newman, in her introduction to Hildegard's *Scivias*, has observed that "our era has created the image of Hildegard the feminist, the liberationist, the 'creation-centered mystic,' the wholistic health practitioner, the prophet of ecological justice."[24] A footnote suggests that this stereotype has been promulgated by the publications of Bear and Company, publishers of Matthew Fox and his Institute in Culture and Creation Spirituality.[25]

Fox, his publishers, and his institute are to be credited with bringing many of the mystics' texts to light, making them available to a wider public. Fox's emphasis on the goodness and blessedness of creation and on comparative spirituality is a welcome corrective for many who find "traditional" Christianity too much focused on sin and brokenness. In *Original Blessing*, Fox seeks to debunk what he calls "Creation, Fall, and Redemption theology," blaming Augustine for introducing the notion of original sin.[26] In his later works, Fox finds resources for creation spirituality among Native Americans, liberation theologians, ecologists, feminists, and Jungians.[27] While Fox's emphasis on blessedness gives his creation spirituality wide appeal, its optimistic reading of the tradition, including the mystical tradition, and of human nature seems a bit too rosy at times.

Christian Ecofeminism

Christian feminists have, for a long time, seen a connection between the oppression of women and the oppression of nature. Rosemary Ruether, in a programmatic essay, traced a dialectic between a wholistic, communal, earth-based religiosity and a more competitive, imperialistic civilization.[28] While Christianity eventually identified with the latter urge, the oppression of both women and the earth predated Christianity, in Ruether's view. Women, she says, "have...been identified with nature, the earth, and the body in its despised and rejected form," and must become "the spokesmen [*sic*] for a new humanity arising out of the reconciliation of spirit and body" (51).

Ruether lays the groundwork for much Christian feminist theology, including that seeking to address issues of ecology and faith.[29] She sets the agenda for a "revolution of the feminine [that]...does not merely reject the spirit child born from the earth but seeks to reclaim spirit for body and body for spirit in a messianic appearing of the body of God" (52). This notion of the world as God's body provides an organic model that resonates with Hebraic thinking, with the

Christian tradition, and with those of us who hope to overcome the hierarchical dualism that has devalued women and their bodies and disembodied God's very Spirit.[30]

Panentheism

Not only feminist theologians but process thinkers, too, have struggled to speak more positively of the relationship between creator and creation, between body and spirit, between mind and matter. Pantheism, the idea that nature and God are identical, obliterates the distinction between creation and creator.[31] Process theology uses the term *panentheism* to speak of God's relation to the created world as "in" everything but not identical with it.[32] The approach I have taken, in which we see God's Spirit as present and evident in the ongoing processes of creation, bears much in common with panentheism, but it finds this relatedness in the Bible without recourse to Whitehead's process philosophy.

Marjorie Suchocki, in *The Fall to Violence*, demonstrates her reliance on Whitehead's thought, but she has chosen to refer to her theology as "relational" rather than "process."[33] In this book she grapples with the doctrine of sin taught by the likes of Augustine and Niebuhr, drawing from the critiques of both feminist and process theologians. Her definition of sin is both realistic and relational: "Sin is the violation of creation, and therefore a rebellion against creation's well-being. Insofar as creation involves God as creator, sin also entails a violation against God" (16). Marjorie Suchocki has, I believe, employed a theological model that seeks to promote the well-being and right relations of God, creation, and creature; hers is a creation-centered spirituality and one that affirms both the brokenness and the possibility of creaturely existence.

Seeing the Spirit

In a sense, this chapter has been as much about creation and human nature as it has been about the Holy Spirit and spirituality, and yet in systemic theology it is difficult, if not impossible, to avoid such connections. Rather than presenting a theological method at the outset, an interpretive model has been employed and laid out along the way. Creation and scripture, nature and revelation, are intertwined. By searching the Bible with an eye to greenness, a pattern revealed itself. By watching the garden grow and witnessing the dance of springtime, the meaning of scripture sprouted and took root. My Reformed self wanted always to dig in the soil of scripture; my Celtic self looks for evidence in lived life. Both Calvin and Coleridge teach us to see the Bible always as a clarifying lens rather than as an end in itself and to trust the one Spirit who dwells in script and soul alike.

The Spirit of greenness is visible in a way that transcends metaphor, analogy, and imagery. The Creativity that causes leaves to unfold and buds to flower *is* the Creator Spirit, the One who broods over creation still. Both books—nature and the Bible—reveal the blessedness and the brokenness of creation. Rose-colored glasses filter out the very real violence in human hearts and in the forces of nature. Nature displays God's imagination and exuberance, the Spirit's extravagance and fecundity, the Word's generosity and relevance. In growing greenness, God's Spirited Word is visible, incarnate.

Reflection on scripture and creation, on lived life and ecstatic vision, bring focus to the triune God. The Spirit creates, the Word sanctifies, the Mother suffers. In our meanderings, God's Spirit has been seen as life-giving, renewing, refreshing, as healing, restoring, reconciling. The creating Spirit is also the pruning, winnowing Spirit, the one who plants *and* plucks up. God's Spirit animates and chastens the created order and makes a home among earthlings, *adamah,* takes root and grows in fertile souls.

And so pneumatology is also spirituality, for the life of the Spirit in the world is in relatedness to creatures. We are growing into right relationship with God and with creation by means of the Spirit's cultivation in our lives. God's Spirit seeks a form, an abode, and finds it in creation, as surely as exiles long for home. Right relationship, righteousness, has to do with spiritual health and well-being—ours, our neighbors', creation's, and God's. When creation suffers, God suffers. Spirituality has to do with all of these connections, not only with the interior life of human beings.

Those who have lost the sense of sight can teach the sighted about seeing. We seers take things for granted, and we are adept at overlooking what we don't wish to see. Annie Dillard tells of those who were blind as they learn to see again. She longs to see what they see: "Eden before Adam gave names. The scales would drop from my eyes; I'd see trees like men walking; I'd run down the road against all orders, hallooing and leaping."[34] God's greening Spirit enables us to see anew, as the blind recovering their sight, as newlysighted souls, lost in wonder.

Spring is pretty well in force now. The tulips and daffodils have spent themselves and the daylilies and irises are a ways off. The awe is wearing off bit by bit. We who see can take a lesson from blind poets, from Bartimaeus and Saul. The newness, the childlike awe, the wide-eyed wonder of original blessedness, of olive branch and rainbow, of finding what was once lost—this is the work of the Spirit. So also the falling away of scales, the removal of logs and splinters, the turning of our gaze to the weak and the lonely, the sick of heart and body— these also are the Spirit's doing.

Desire, Denial, Delight

Satisfaction

We got up at the crack of dawn, perhaps before dawn broke. An assortment of friends from church, we drove north from our homes in Southern California, up through the high desert, along the foothills of the High Sierra. Our immediate goal was the town of Independence, just north of Mount Whitney, the highest point in California and in the continental U.S., where we would turn up into the mountains to find our trailhead. We parked the cars, put on our heavy socks, tied up our boots, filled our water bottles, donned our packs, and set off up the trail, the key word being "up."

There is something very freeing about hiking with a pack on your back, knowing you have everything needed—actually more than is needed—to survive in the wilderness for a few days. I was younger and fitter then, but I still remember the effort it took, emotional and physical, to walk up and up, through wooded glens, along rocky passageways on all fours at time and, just when the pass was in sight, an hour's worth of switchbacks along the face of the cliff.

The view from the top of Kearsarge Pass was breathtaking, and the satisfaction of having reached that vantage point was exhilarating. We could see where we'd come from, even as far as the highway and the glitter of cars; we could see our goal for the night, a mountain lake nestled in the valley below and snowcapped Whitney to the south. All our senses were piqued, along with all our yearnings. We noticed the wildflowers growing out of the rocks, smelled the pine trees, felt the breeze on our faces, heard the chatter of birds, and tasted the cool water—never did water taste so good.

Walking down the other side was harder than we'd imagined, working against gravity and the pull of the valley below. We were dusty and sweaty, exhausted and hungry, when we reached our lakeside camp. I remember jumping into icy water and feeling fresh, clean, relaxed. A meal cooked by campstove tasted like a feast after a day of trail mix. Was it camper's stew or chili? Were there crackers and sardines? Had someone packed a bottle of wine? Who knows? But it satisfied our hungry bodies, and we enjoyed laughter and good company before we fell into an exhausted sleep.

I've never been one for athletics or asceticism, but this journey, this feeling of being pushed to the limits, of deep hunger and deep satisfaction, helps me to understand how intimately connected are the hungers of soul and body. Rarely, if ever, am I so hungry, so thirsty, that I must eat to live, to function. We are more often, we well-fed Americans, sated than starving, and though the work of a pastor/teacher can be tiring at times, there is hardly ever the physical exhaustion of those who work with their hands and bodies to make a living.

I find beautiful irony in the fact that the very things we need to survive are often pleasant and enjoyable—food, drink, exercise, sleep, friendship, sex. Desire for these things is part of the created order. Yet how twisted and confused are those very desires when they become excessive, compulsive, abusive, addictive. Bodily desire, the longings of our flesh, are not inherently evil, as certain Christian traditions have taught. Our bodies are earthen vessels, a home for God's Spirit; what Paul calls "the flesh," *sarx,* is desire gone wrong. *Sarx* and *soma,* flesh and body, are not exactly the same thing. Yet how easily the two have become confused, our bodies—especially women's bodies—being blamed for all kinds of evil.

The spiritual life is a life of desire and fulfillment, longing and joy. As spiritual creatures we long for home, for God's Spirit, for the gifts of God's good pleasure. Yet all too often we seek to fill this longing with that which is not God, to sate our appetites with too much of a good thing, with distractions that will help us deny our real emptiness. Food and drink are central to biblical faith, to both Judaism and Christianity. Living water, bread of life, wine of gladness, these represent the Spirit's ability to satisfy our deepest desires, to heal our wounds, to nurture the life of faith. And yet the Bible knows also of desire gone wrong, of the fine line between longing and idolatry.

We had a light breakfast but were never allowed a midday meal on Thanksgiving. The anticipatory preparations of the day were meant somehow to whet our appetites for the feast that would come. By lunchtime the turkey smells were beginning to fill the house. The dining room table was set with great care and beauty, with silver and china, with linens and candles, flowers and hand-lettered placecards. Sometimes there were pilgrim hats or Indian bonnets for the children and special treats for the pets. There were relish trays and nut cups. As the day progressed, the preparations became more furious. Usually the turkey came out of the oven just as all the guests arrived and the final frenzy began. Dad carved the turkey, but he usually needed several helpers—to remove the stuffing, to taste the little chunks that fell off the bones, to mop up the juice. Mom managed everything else: getting the plates warm, keeping the many side dishes—peas, potatoes, yams, green beans, Grandma Prichard's crescent rolls—hot and ready to serve. Others shuttled things like butter and jam and cranberries and serving spoons onto the table. While all this was going on, I made the gravy according to rubrics set forth by my maternal grandmother, Alice. When the moment arrived, we stood around the table and sang our family blessing:

How good is the Lord we adore, our faithful, unchangeable Friend,

Whose love is as great as his power and knows neither measure nor end.

Tis Jesus the first and the last, whose Spirit shall guide us safe home.

We'll praise him for all that is past, and trust him for all that shall come.[1]

Celebratory feasting is part of all cultures (including my own obviously White, Anglo-Saxon Protestant culture!), and the food and the stories and the legends differ from family to family, but food, special food, delicious food, has the power of connecting us to one another and to the Spirit of creation. At thanksgiving feasts we literally "delight ourselves in fatness" (Isa. 55:2, RSV), while trying to remember those who go hungry most of the time. Holy people of all times and places have learned that bodily hunger can help pique our hunger for God and give us a greater appreciation for more simple meals. Yet voluntary poverty, as in ascetic fasting or simple living, is a freely chosen hunger, a hunger millions in the world can't choose. Our abundance and their hunger are deeply connected, a spiritual crisis for all of us, but often unrecognized, unacknowledged.

Hunger for God

There are at least three kinds of hunger in the Bible—common hunger for daily bread, the deep hunger of famine and poverty, and a hunger for God's presence. The three are connected. Our hunger for daily bread is met by God's provision and the work of our hands. Genuine gratitude for such provision moves us to acknowledge the poor, the hungry, the thirsty, and to seek ways to participate in God's provision for them as well. God promises to fulfill our deepest desires, to be present to us as spiritual food: "O taste and see that the LORD is good" (Ps. 34:8); "Blessed are those who hunger and thirst for righteousness, for they will be filled" (Mt. 5:6). Even as we long for God, we long for justice, for the health and well-being of all creation that the Spirit prepares.

Throughout scripture the faithful are taught to be content, satisfied with sufficiency rather than greedy for excess. The primal story of creation and sin centers on food; God provides all kinds of trees with fruit for human consumption, but the man and the woman become desirous of the forbidden fruit, the fruit that will make them like God (Gen. 2:16–17; 3:1–7). God provides manna and quail for the freed slaves wandering in the wilderness—no more, no less than they need for daily sustenance (Ex. 16). Jesus teaches the disciples to live in dependence on God, to pray for daily bread (Mt. 6:11), to trust God who feeds even the birds of the air (Mt. 6:25–26), and that hoarding is foolish (Lk. 12:13–21). Paul values contentment: "I know what it is to have little, and I know what it is to have plenty" (Phil. 4:12).

Throughout scripture we sense also the presence of the poor, of famine and drought, of injustice and wrong relations. During hard times Esau sold his birthright for a pot of stew (Gen. 25:29–34). Israel was sold into slavery in Egypt during a time of famine and drought (Gen. 47:20–21; Ex. 1:1–14). The law of Moses provided for the poor, the widow, and the alien by means such as gleaning, whereby landowners were required to leave the edges of their fields unharvested for the hungry (Lev. 19:9–10; 23:22; Deut. 24:19–22). Both the law and the prophets urged care for the poor, underscored with the refrain: "Remember that you were a slave in Egypt and the LORD your God redeemed you from there; therefore I command you to do this" (Deut. 24:18), and again, "Remember that you were a slave in the land of Egypt; therefore I am commanding you to do this" (v. 22). Isaiah links Israel's satisfaction with a willingness to show mercy and justice:

> If you offer your food to the hungry
> and satisfy the needs of the afflicted,
> then your light shall rise in the darkness
> and your gloom be like the noonday.
> The LORD will guide you continually,
> and satisfy your needs in parched places,
> and make your bones strong;
> and you shall be like a watered garden,
> like a spring of water,
> whose waters never fail. (Isa. 58:10–11)

Jesus' prophetic message confirms this theme: "I was hungry and you gave me food, I was thirsty and you gave me something to drink, I was a stranger and you welcomed me" (Mt. 25:35).

At times spiritual and physical desire become indistinguishable. In the Psalms, the law of God and the fear of the Lord are sweet:

> More to be desired are they than gold,
> even much fine gold;
> sweeter also than honey,
> and drippings of the honeycomb. (Ps. 19:10)

God's word itself becomes appetizing: "How sweet are your words to my taste, sweeter than honey to my mouth!" (Ps. 119:103). The longing for God becomes almost sensual:

My soul is satisfied as with a rich feast,
  and my mouth praises you with joyful lips
when I think of you on my bed,
  and meditate on you in the watches of the night.
                                        (Ps. 63:5–6)

Delight in God transforms and satisfies all desires: "Take delight in the LORD, and [God] will give you the desires of your heart" (Ps. 37:4). When Mary, in her canticle of praise to God, sings "[God] has filled the hungry with good things, and sent the rich away empty" (Lk. 1:53), the distinction between bodily hunger and spiritual satisfaction is gone.[2] Justice and spirituality are intimately connected.

Feasting and Fasting

Eating and celebration go together, as do fasting and repentance. A festal calendar was established for Israel, setting forth feasts and festivals of thanksgiving (Deut. 16:1–17; Ex. 23:14–17; 34:18–24, Lev. 23, Num. 28—29); such festivals were also the occasion for sharing God's blessings with the poor. The law provided as well for public fasting on the Day of Atonement (Lev. 16:29–34; 23:26–32; Num. 29:7). Private fasts were encouraged for repentance, lamentation, mourning, supplication. The prophets put both feasting and fasting into perspective, noting that either could be abused or excessive.

Great feasts, full of eating and drinking and dancing, are occasions for celebration and severity throughout scripture. The first Passover (Ex. 12) was a solemn meal of deliverance, which developed into a great feast of remembering (2 Chr. 30, 35). Belshazzar's Feast became an occasion for God's voice of judgment to be heard (Dan. 5). The feasting of Ahasueras in Esther sets the stage for divine intervention. A wedding feast in Cana of Galilee is the setting for Jesus' first miracle (Jn. 2:1–11). Another feast provides the gruesome scene for the beheading of John the Baptist (Mt. 14:1–12; Mk. 6:14–29).

There are also eschatological feasts in the Bible, calling the faithful into a hopeful future of celebration and satisfaction. Isaiah invites the hungry and thirsty to a great banquet celebrating the end of exile:

Ho, everyone who thirsts,
  come to the waters;
and you that have no money,
  come, buy and eat!

Come, buy wine and milk
    without money and without price.
Why do you spend your money for that which is not bread,
    and your labor for that which does not satisfy?
Listen carefully to me, and eat what is good,
    and delight yourselves in rich food. (Isa. 55:1–2)

Jesus' parables urge the faithful to prepare for a great feast to come (Mt. 25:1–13), a marriage banquet where the poor and needy will be welcome (Mt. 22:1–10; Lk. 14:15–24), to practice the etiquette of humility when invited to a wedding (Lk. 14:7–14). A great feast is prepared when the prodigal son returns home (Lk. 15:11–32). In the end the faithful will be invited to the marriage supper of the Lamb (Rev.19:9).

The practice of fasting was more often private than public, signifying remorse for sin, mourning the dead, lamentation for loss. The prophets, like Jesus, condemned hypocritical fasting: "When you fasted and lamented in the fifth month and in the seventh, for these seventy years, was it for me that you fasted? And when you eat and when you drink, do you not eat and drink only for yourselves?" (Zech. 7:5–6). Isaiah, too, speaks of false and true fasting:

"Why do we fast, but you do not see?
    Why humble ourselves, but you do not notice?"
Look, you serve your own interest on your fast day,
    and oppress all your workers.

Is not this the fast that I choose:
    to loose the bonds of injustice,
    to undo the thongs of the yoke,
    to let the oppressed go free,
    and to break every yoke?
Is it not to share your bread with the hungry,
    and bring the homeless poor into your house;
when you see the naked, to cover them,
    and not to hide yourself from your own kin?
                         (Isa. 58:3, 6–7)

Following his baptism, Jesus fasted in the wilderness for forty days as a preparation for ministry, but, like the prophets before him, Jesus condemned the hypocrisy of false fasting (Mt. 6:16–18). When asked why his disciples did not fast, Jesus likened himself to a bridegroom, his disciples to guests at a wedding feast (Mt. 9:14–17; Mk. 2:18–22; Lk. 5:33–39). Food is the focus of both gratitude and longing; spiritual satisfaction is tied to the appetites and desires of both *nephesh* and *basar*. God's indwelling Spirit transforms and sanctifies our hunger, moving us from greed and idolatry to justice and generosity.

Water, Wine, and Bread of Life

The life of faith, this spiritual trek of longing and satisfaction, of desire and fulfillment, has at its center very real objects of desire, earthly elements that have become sacred signs of the Spirit's sanctifying, satisfying presence. Our hunger for God and for God's pleasures is conveyed by biblical imagination in many ways, as we have seen. God's word and law are likened to sweet honey; the Spirit's presence is our home, our resting place; God is our faithful spouse, Jesus the bridegroom; Jesus calls us friends and offers us his very self for sustenance and refreshment.

In the biblical tradition and in Christian practice, a number of elemental symbols take on sacred power as they communicate the rich layers of meaning that constitute the divine/human relationship. Water, wine, and bread hold sacred meaning for both Jewish and Christian faith, evoking as they do our basic need for sustenance and our deepest longings and appetites. The Christian sacraments, particularly communion and baptism, draw their meaning from the rich symbolism of these earthy and biblical elements—water of life, wine of gladness, bread of heaven.

Along with manna and quail, God provided water from the rock of Horeb (Ex. 17), quenching the thirst of the wilderness wanderers, the same folk who had passed safely through the waters of the Red Sea. Water is both the gateway to a land of promise and a means of survival, "a way in the wilderness and rivers in the desert" (Isa. 43:19). The psalmist pants for God as a deer longs for flowing streams (Ps. 42:1) yet seeks God's deliverance from thunder of cataracts, waves, and billows (v. 7). The prophet Ezekiel envisions a sacred river, flowing freely, giving life, suggestive of the river of life in the heavenly city (Ezek. 47:1–2; Rev. 22).

Jesus is baptized in the waters of the Jordan, an event tied vividly to the presence of the Holy Spirit (Mt. 3:13–17; Mk. 1:9–11; Lk. 3:21–22). Hence, water, as the primal element in Christian baptism, calls to mind cleansing, death, and resurrection, new birth, initiation, but also God's covenantal faithfulness, our adoption as children of God, and the infilling of the Spirit. Jesus' thirst mirrors our own; he is thirsty on the cross (Jn. 19:28–30), and he identifies himself with all who hunger and thirst (Mt. 25:31–46). Jesus asks the woman at the well for a drink, and in the midst of that revealing encounter, he declares himself to be living water: "Everyone who drinks of this water will be thirsty again, but those who drink of the water that I will give them will never be thirsty. The water that I will give will become in them a spring of water gushing up to eternal life" (Jn. 4:13–14). Jesus invites the thirsty to come to him and to be filled with rivers of living water, a sign of the giving of the Spirit (Jn. 7:37–39). At the wedding feast of the Lamb, the heavenly banquet, all thirst will be satisfied at last:

> The Spirit and the bride say, "Come."
> And let everyone who hears say, "Come."
> And let everyone who is thirsty come.
> Let anyone who wishes take the water of life as a gift. (Rev. 22:17)

Scripture bears witness to the dangerous qualities of wine as well as to its enjoyment. Noah planted a vineyard, but he became drunk at times (Gen. 9:21). The fruit of the vine can be wild and sour (Isa. 5:1–7; Jer. 31:27–30) as well as sweet and gladdening (Ps. 104:13; Isa. 55:1). Wine and its power to intoxicate can signify God's wrath and judgment (Ps. 60:3; Isa. 63:3–6; Rev. 14:10). The wine of the Passover seder signifies both the plagues on Egypt and the expectation of peace and justice. Wine is seen as a gift from God, a blessing that enhances life's pleasure when taken in gratitude and joy, overflowing grace (Ps. 23:5), but a mocker (Prov. 20:1) when taken in excess.

Jesus turns the water of purification into fine wine of celebration, despite the apparent inebriation of the guests at the wedding (Jn. 2:10). He speaks of his presence as like unto new wine, requiring new wineskins (Mt. 9:16–17; Mk. 2:21–22; Lk. 5:36–39). At the last supper, Jesus speaks also of himself as the vine, God the vinedresser, his disciples as branches, called to bear fruit through a mutually dependent relationship, an abiding in one another (Jn. 15:1–11). Jesus speaks of his death as a "cup" that must be swallowed despite the suffering it represents (Mt. 26:39; Mk. 14:36; Lk. 22:42). The cup of the Passover meal he shared with his friends he calls "my blood of the

covenant, which is poured out for many for the forgiveness of sins"
(Mt. 26:28; cf. Mk. 14:24; Lk. 22:20). Like fine wine, the Spirit is
intoxicating. At Pentecost, the disciples are thought to be drunk with
new wine, their exuberance and glossolalia striking the crowd as anything but sober (Acts 2:13, 15). Paul urges the saints not to be drunk
with wine but to be filled with the Holy Spirit (Eph. 5:18).

God provides daily bread for the faithful, from manna in the
wilderness to the bread of the presence, from multiplied loaves to
bread of life. Abraham urges Sarah to quickly bake bread cakes for
three unexpected visitors, thus showing hospitality to strangers and
to God (Gen. 18). The freed slaves had no time for their bread to rise
as they hurriedly left Egypt (Ex. 12:33–34). David and his friends
were given the holy bread by a priest when they were hungry, an
incident Jesus used to interpret the laws about the Sabbath (1 Sam.
21:1–6; Mk. 2:23–28).

Jesus' feeding miracles are told in each gospel (Mt. 14:13–21;
15:32–39; Mk. 6:30–44; Mk. 8:1–10; Lk. 9:10–17; Jn. 6:1–13). In
the Fourth Gospel, Jesus is seen as embodying the signs and wonders
he performs; he heals a blind man (Jn. 9) and says, "I am the light of
the world"; he raises Lazarus (Jn. 11) and says, "I am the resurrection
and the life"; he feeds the hungry multitude and says, "I am the bread
of life. Whoever comes to me will never be hungry, and whoever
believes in me will never be thirsty" (Jn. 6:35). "Those who eat my
flesh and drink my blood have eternal life" (v. 54). On the road to
Emmaus, Jesus' friends do not recognize him, but when they share a
meal with him, "their eyes were opened and they recognized him" in
the breaking of the bread (Lk. 24:30–31).

And so the feasts and the fasts of the Jewish faith and the sacraments and the celebrations of the Christian tradition are times when
we remember the connections, when we *re*-member the links between
bodily and spiritual hunger, between God's freely flowing grace and
our vocation of hospitality, between our satiety and the world's hunger.
Water, wine, and bread appeal to the sense of taste, to the appetites
and desires of both body and soul. Walking that fine line between
gratitude and gluttony, between denial and denigration, between
enjoyment and idolatry, this is the challenge of life in the Spirit.

Desert Spirituality

Roberta Bondi, in writing on the desert spirituality, claims, "The
root of all prayer, indeed all life itself, is desire for God."[3] By focusing

on godly desire, on the longing for a deep and intimate friendship with God, Bondi seeks to make sense of the teachings of the desert mothers and fathers, teachings both strange and fascinating to our twentieth-century tastes.[4] Teresa Shaw, in a magistral study, also seeks a slant on early Christian asceticism that draws connections between spiritual and bodily health.[5] Rather than a triumph of spirit over matter, a taming of the "lower" appetites of the body, Shaw understands asceticism "as a way of life that requires daily discipline and intentionality in bodily behaviors."[6] *Askesis* was not unique to Christianity; it described the rigorous discipline of an athlete whose physical training had also a spiritual dimension. Just so, the martyrs and monastics of the early church were considered athletes of the faith, their rigors both physical and spiritual.

Christians in North Africa and Palestine fled to the desert even before the Emperor Constantine embraced the faith and put an end to the persecutions. Some fled to the desert to escape martyrdom, others to prepare themselves for it.[7] When the persecutions ended, the red martyrdom of massacre became the white martyrdom of monasticism. Some early monks, like Athanasius of Alexandria, champion of the Nicene faith, fled to the desert in exile when their theological ideas fell out of favor. Athanasius' *Life of Antony,* a prototype for later hagiographies, described the call of the desert in a form that beckoned to many.[8]

It was not hard to find support in scripture for the desert spirituality. Hebrew prophets, notably Elijah, lived apart in the wilderness. Jesus went into the desert, praying, fasting, and wrestling with evil as a prelude to his ministry. The command to sell all possessions, to give to the poor, and to follow were taken seriously by Antony and others.[9] Though these fathers and mothers lived alone (anchorites) or in small groups (cenobites), they worked with their hands, gave to the poor, and performed various works of ministry—"healing the sick, casting out demons…comforting the sorrowful, reconciling those at variance, urging all to put nothing in the world before the love of Christ."[10]

The *Apophthegmata,* or "Sayings of the Desert Fathers [and Mothers]," were collected and written in the fifth century in Skete, Egypt, a time when the founders of the movement were fading in memory.[11] The "Sayings" are full of wise words about a variety of spiritual virtues, and they include many anecdotes about the vanquishing of hunger, thirst, and sexual desire.[12]

Moderation is valued: Amma (a title for "mother") Syncletica urged "perfect temperance."[13] Divine asceticism is distinguished from demonic, she says, "through its quality of balance."[14] Hospitality is encouraged: "All the years he stayed with us, we gave him a little enough measure of food for the year. And every time we came to visit him, he shared it with us."[15] Charity is seen as more important than strict fasting:

> Once two brethren came to a certain elder whose custom it was not to eat every day. But when he saw the brethren he invited them with joy to dine with him, saying: "Fasting has its reward, but he who eats out of charity fulfills two commandments, for he sets aside his own will and he refreshes his hungry brethren."[16]

Sometimes, their asceticism strikes us as excessive:

> It was said of an old man that one day he wanted a small fig. Taking one, he held it up in front of his eyes, and not being overcome by his desire, he repented, reproaching himself for even having had this wish.[17]

All bodily appetites, including anger, wealth, fame, home, and lust, are seats of struggle: "This is the truth, if a monk regards contempt as praise, poverty as riches, and hunger as a feast, he will never die."[18] Sexual desire is a problem for both the Ammas and the Abbas (a title for "fathers"); Amma Sarah was said to have waged battle with "the demon of fornication" for thirteen years.[19] As for the Abbas, lust often took on a female form:

> A brother was severely tempted by the demon of lust. In fact, four demons, under the appearance of very beautiful women, spent forty days attacking him to bring him to the shame of intercourse. But he fought courageously and was not overcome, and seeing his successful warfare, God allowed him to experience no more the flames of sensuality.[20]

All females have the power to tempt: "On a journey a monk met some nuns and when he saw them he turned aside off the road. The abbess said to him: 'If you had been a perfect monk, you would not have looked so closely as to see that we were women.'"[21] The desire for sexual pleasure is as evil as indulging it:

Many, tempted by bodily pleasures, do not defile their bodies but, committing fornication in thought, they are fornicators in their souls while preserving their bodies unstained. So it is good, my friends, to do that which is written, that each one should guard his heart with care.[22]

Ironically, the desert, the scene of spiritual struggle, is seen also as a refuge from temptation:

Abraham, the disciple of Abbot Sisois, said to him: Father, you are an old man. Let's go back to the world. Abbot Sisois replied: Very well, we'll go where there are no women. His disciple said: What is the place in which there are no women, except the desert alone? The elder replied to him: Therefore take me into the desert.[23]

It is this struggle with desire, with hunger and lust, that presents a theological problem for an embodied spirituality, for a theology of the Spirit that seeks to affirm earthly pleasure. As Shaw and others have pointed out, a negative meaning has been attached to the terms *body* and *flesh*.[24] We have seen that there is a tendency to confuse Paul's use of the term "flesh," or *sarx*, with all things bodily, with *soma*. We have also seen that in Christian asceticism, there has been a temptation to divorce the spiritual from the somatic, seeing the former as more valuable than the latter. Here is where hierarchical dualism enters in, not in speaking in parallel terms but in privileging the one over the other, in drawing distinctions so tightly that they become antithetical rather than complementary.

Twice I took weeklong retreats at St. Andrew's Priory, a Benedictine monastery in the high desert of Southern California. Growing up Protestant, I had never encountered Roman Catholic spirituality at such close range. Though we had our own retreat program, we took part in the rhythms of Benedictine life—the long silence, the daily offices, midday mass. We witnessed firsthand the living of the motto *ora / labora*, work and prayer, prayer and work, discovering that the two became indistinguishable in the social and liturgical intercourse of the monastery. We shared meals and conversations with the monks and were lucky enough to be there on the Feast of the Transfiguration. Noontime mass that day was followed by a great and plenteous Mexican banquet—I can still taste the handmade tamales. We were recipients of Benedictine hospitality, welcome strangers.

Asceticism doesn't have to be unbalanced, dualistic, disparaging of the pleasures of life. The monks in the desert knew the connection between body and soul. Like us, friends and followers expected Antony to be emaciated or weak with hunger but marveled at his physical fitness, even after twenty years of seclusion: "When they beheld him, they were amazed to see that his body had maintained its former condition, neither fat from lack of exercise, nor emaciated from fasting and combat with demons, but was just as they had known him prior to his withdrawal."[25] Even to the end of his life, Antony was seen to be fit both spiritually and physically, a fitness Chitty sees as "against all types of dualism."[26]

Holy Hunger

The monastic movement was born in the desert. Benedict of Nursia modeled his monastic colonies on the Egyptian precedent; his *Rule* was composed less than a hundred years after the *Apophthegmata* began to circulate.[27] Just as the desert was both site of struggle and safe haven, so the monastery became a place apart, a home where holy hunger could be nurtured. Nuns and monks of all ages have struggled to practice an asceticism that honors body and soul, contemplation and action, hunger and holiness. Some have found that balance, at least on occasion, but many medieval monastics took asceticism to daunting extremes.

In her book *Holy Feast and Holy Fast*, Carolyn Walker Bynum provides us with a fascinating and provocative study of the ways spirituality and food are connected in the Christian faith, particularly in the lives of religious women in the High Middle Ages.[28] Fasting, eucharistic theology, and female piety are explored in depth. Reflecting on some of the eucharistic prayers of the church, Bynum observes a shift in emphasis from the early into the medieval, which is particularly germane as we explore bodily and spiritual hunger. Cyprian's words, Bynum suggests, are typical of the early church's emphasis on bread of heaven:

> The body of the Lord cannot be flour alone or water alone, unless both should be united and joined together and completed in the mass of one bread; in which very sacrament our people are shown to be made one, so that in like manner as many grains, collected, and ground, and mixed together into

one mass, make one bread; so in Christ who is the heavenly bread, we may know that there is one body, with which our number is joined and united.[29]

Whereas the early church found the unity of the body of Christ, the Church, in the one loaf, "the bread of heaven...was replaced in late medieval hymns, poems, and paintings by the flesh of Christ, ripped open and spilling forth pulsating streams of insistent, scarlet blood, to wash and feed the individual hungry soul."[30]

This move, from bread of heaven to body broken, for Bynum, reflects also a shift in female spirituality, leading to a deep and vicarious identification with Christ's bodily suffering. This breaking of Christ's body, in communion and in the church, is also a breaking of the wholeness of soul and body, a breaking that amplifies all kinds of dualism. While spiritual and bodily health might have been connected in early asceticism, medieval holiness often seems to mean a breaking of the body in favor of the spirit. While this shift is gradual and subtle, and while calls for balance persisted, Bynum links this shift with the increase of hierarchical dualism in the church, including the growing separation between the priesthood and the people, a contrivance of "church architecture, liturgical practice, and priestly power."[31]

It could be said that excess typifies both feasting and fasting in the High Middle Ages. Bynum draws upon culinary history to speak about the sensual aspects of medieval eating. "The feast," she says, "was a banquet for all the senses; indeed, food was almost an excuse for indulging senses other than taste."[32] This sensuality carried over to eucharistic devotion: "It rang with the music of bells, glowed with light, dissolved on the tongue into honeycomb or bloody flesh, and announced its presence, when profaned or secreted away, by leaving a trail of blood."[33]

Because the sense of taste was rarely engaged literally (the priests "receiving" on behalf of the people), hunger itself became excessive. The people abstained from the eucharist out of awe and fear, and mystics abstained from daily bread, whetting their appetites for the host and for ecstatic sharing in Christ's suffering. Holy women took fasting to extremes, despite warnings for moderation.[34] Though fasting was a moderated abstinence in the liturgical cycles of the church, women, seen as more carnal, had more to overcome in their bodies. So women mystics began to desire not only the eucharist as literal food, but their desire for Christ's wounds becomes at times erotic.

It is clear that many medieval mystics, male and female, took abstinence of all kinds to great extremes and that bodily abstinence was meant to heighten spiritual hunger. Chastity heightened desire for God as lover, a spirituality typified by the *Brautmystik* and the emphasis among mystical writers on the Song of Songs.[35] Physical hunger magnified spiritual hunger, and holy women may be considered experts in this regard.[36] Though the texts and stories of any number of medieval women could be used to exemplify this trend, the life and writing of Catherine of Siena will be considered briefly.[37]

The reader of Catherine's *Dialogue,* a conversation between the mystic and her God, is struck by the central theme of holy desire. The mystic's desire for God grows throughout the work; she is intoxicated with the Spirit, longing fervently for union with Christ and his suffering. God's desire for relationship with all the saints is mirrored in the saint's desire for God. Spiritual longing is not just for her own sanctification but for love of neighbor as well. Catherine's imagery is varied and sensate. Divine/human relationship is described as bridge, sun, lamp, garden, vineyard, wine cellar, rooted tree, ship, medicine, mother, and child.[38] The mystic's theology is rooted in scripture and in the teachings of Augustine, Anselm, Aquinas, Athanasius. Yet she dares to offer a critique of holy mother church, a church deeply divided by the Avignon papacy, the so-called Babylonian Captivity.

Catherine speaks over and over again of the pleasures of the senses and of the body, pleasures that are meant for good but are often open to evil. The body's senses are gates that "open up, as instruments that respond to the soul" (299). Though this earthly body is "heavy" and will ultimately rise to new life, suffering and sanctification take place in embodied, incarnate existence: "I am speaking of sacrifice both in act and in spirit joined together as the vessel is joined with the water offered to one's lord. For the water cannot be presented without the vessel" (46). Despite the excesses to which Catherine appeared to have taken her abstinence, her writing holds soul and body together; as the two natures of Christ were united for our salvation, so flesh and spirit struggle together in us.

Catherine's mystical theology, her christology, and her spirituality of desire come together in her eucharistic devotion. She longs to eat at "the table of the teaching of Christ crucified" (141), to feed on the souls of those won to salvation by Christ's suffering:

And after she has chewed them she tastes the flavor, savoring the fruit of her labor and the delight of this food of souls, enjoying its taste in the fire of charity for me and her neighbors. And so this food reaches the stomach (that is, the heart), which has been prepared by desire and hunger for souls to receive it willingly, with heartfelt charity and affection for others. (140–141)

Catherine speaks often of the "abyss of charity," Christ's love for us, mysteriously revealed in communion bread, revealed to bodily senses and spiritual sensitivity: "This eye sees in that whiteness the divine nature joined with the human; wholly God, wholly human; the body, soul, and blood of Christ, his soul united with his body and his body and soul united with my divine nature, never straying from me" (210). "The body tastes only the flavor of the bread, but the soul tastes me, God and human" (211).

In the final section, Catherine's *Dialogue* with God becomes autobiographical, as she reveals her own hunger for communion at a time when the laity rarely received it.[39] Catherine tells how she was able to receive the host in miraculous ways, even during a time when she was abstaining from food altogether. God speaks:

The Holy Spirit whom I in my goodness have given, stands ready to serve the soul, he will inspire some minister to give her this food. And the minister, constrained by my burning charity in this Holy Spirit who pricks his conscience, is then moved to feed that soul's hunger and fulfill her longing. (294)

Catherine died in 1380 at the age of thirty-three, having eaten nothing but the host for many months. The record of her life and death together with her writings tell of a spiritual longing both satisfying and shocking to our sensibilities, both food for thought and cautionary tale.

Protestant Piety

We have observed some of the sea changes that took place in the sixteenth century—social, political, theological, ecclesiastical. These shifts were accompanied by shifts in spirituality and piety, especially among those who identified with various Protestant groups. Luther's watchwords, *sola scriptura, sola fide, sola gratia,* encapsulate important challenges to medieval authority, theology, and piety. Though social and political upheaval shook the hierarchical foundations of church and state, and though religious and theological upheaval challenged the institutions of priesthood and papacy, the Roman Catholic Church moved into the new age fairly well intact—at least in most places. Theological reformation resulted in reformation also of piety and spirituality among Protestant adherents, and it is to these changes we turn briefly.

Piety and charity were deeply connected in medieval monastery and in Protestant society. Just as the spiritual hunger of the Hebrew people, of the ammas and abbas, and of the medieval mystics fed into acts of charity and hospitality, so Lutherans, Calvinists, and Anabaptists found ways to minister to the poor, the hungry, the sick, and the alien in their various reformations. While medieval Christians practiced charity in the form of seven corporeal, or bodily, virtues (based on Matthew 25), Protestants sought to institutionalize charity in ways that accorded with the theology of grace alone. Luther was critical of medieval alms, viewing them as salvation by works or as a kind of eternal life insurance. In Wittenberg, Geneva, and Strasbourg, charitable works were encouraged as the result rather than the cause of salvation.[40]

Though Calvin spoke at length about self-denial, he was critical of the kind of asceticism associated with medieval practice, and though Calvinism resulted in all kinds of abstemious behavior, thanksgiving for God's blessings was Calvin's stated motivation.[41] Calvin urges moderation in matters such as fasting and celibacy, denouncing clerical celibacy, in particular.[42] This move away from clerical celibacy among Protestants corresponded with changed attitudes toward women. By viewing marriage and sexuality in a more positive light, the Reformers opened the door for new kinds of roles for women in the church. While feminists raise serious doubts about the "liberation" of nuns from the cloister, Protestant women have found ways to exercise some power in the churches of the Reformation.[43]

The power of Protestant women reached new heights in the latter decades of the nineteenth century. While women in the Protestant churches lost the opportunities afforded by the convent, they enjoyed a kind of dominance in the domestic realm. Their holy hunger led them into social reforms rather than mystic visions.[44] The feminization of the private sphere and the masculine domination of the public sphere continue from Greco-Roman times until today, yet nineteenth-century movements for abolition, suffrage, birth control, missions, and temperance were led by powerful Protestant *matrones,* the foremothers of modern feminism.

The temperance movement in general, and the Women's Christian Temperance Union (W.C.T.U.) under the leadership of Frances Willard in particular, provide an intriguing case study for questions of spiritual hunger, female piety, and social virtue. The temperance movement seems an altogether White, Protestant, Anglo-Saxon, and at first, male movement. Respectable Protestant gentlemen signed the pledge against drinking and formed temperance societies. Only in the 1870s, with the Women's Crusade, did the active involvement of women come into its own. Those women who stormed saloons did so in the cause of domestic peace and tranquillity, believing that hardworking Christian men like their husbands would be lured into poverty and dissipation by demon drink. Though the Women's Crusade was short-lived, it gave women a taste of political and social influence, a taste that drew them to organize and led to the birth of the W.C.T.U.

The W.C.T.U. was at first strictly committed to temperance work, to keeping home and family safe from drunkenness and poverty. But with the election of Frances Willard, the W.C.T.U. began to espouse other reform issues as well, including woman's suffrage. It is striking that an issue of personal piety, abstention from alcohol, became the impetus for all kinds of social reforms; the rhetoric of the temperance movement blamed alcohol itself rather than human weakness for the ills of intemperance. There is little in the literature that addresses the inner spiritual battle with temptation posed by drinking.[45]

For women then as now the private was public, the personal political, for men's drinking led also to prostitution, to domestic violence, to poverty, to disruption of both home and work.[46] In *The Politics of Domesticity,* Barbara Leslie Epstein argues that the temperance movement was an attack on masculine culture, a culture viewed as sinful by pious women: "The antagonism toward men and toward masculine values that had led evangelical women to associate femaleness with piety were now translated into the secular terms of temperance."[47] Temperance women sought first to make their homes safe in every way:

As drinking came to be associated with wife beating, neglect, and desertion, and alcohol became the symbol of a strain of masculine hostility to women and the family, temperance became the obvious terrain of women's defense of home, family, and the values associated with that realm.[48]

So the lines between public and private worlds, male and female realms, became ever more neatly drawn. Frances Willard, a Methodist, claimed to seek the full equality of these two realms:

In primitive days we had the matriarchate which means the rule of the mothers, and now for a painfully lengthened period we have had the patriarchate or the rule of the fathers, but we begin to see the dawn of the amphirate or the joint rule of a joint world by the joint forces of its mothers and its fathers.[49]

Such pious protofeminism strikes us as deeply ironic, for it served to reinforce the Victorian values that kept women domesticated, and it seems confused about whether the male is friend or foe. It is clear that many women, including Willard at times, saw their culture as superior to male culture, at least in a moral sense, for they sought not only "home protection," but they wanted to domesticate the world, with activities in every sphere from education to prison reform to health care to labor. In a manual for young girls, Willard lays out her agenda:

The skill in detail, trustworthiness in finance, motherliness in sympathy, so long extolled in private life, shall exalt public station. Indeed, if I were asked the mission of the ideal woman, I would reply: IT IS TO MAKE THE WHOLE WORLD HOMELIKE…She came into the college and elevated it, into literature and hallowed it, into the business world and ennobled it. She will come into government and purify it, into politics and cleanse its Stygian pool, for woman will make homelike every place on this round earth.[50]

Willard led the W.C.T.U. to ever more radical involvements, eventually espousing socialism, though the organization kept its distance from overtly "feminist" activities. Willard remained the group's freely elected president until her death in 1898.

Tastes Differing

The ironies of women's history begin to crystallize in many questions. Is women's experience, including religious experience, different from men's? Is this difference something to be affirmed? Or does the quest for equality call for an equation of male and female in every way? Doesn't the accent on difference simply serve to reinforce traditional stereotypes, thereby reinforcing women's subjugation? It would seem such questions are at the center of feminist discourse, including feminist theological discourse. Some feminists affirm the differences between male and female experience and call for either complementarity or female superiority.[51] There are others who seek to minimize the differences between male and female, fearing that the gender stereotypes of androcentric culture will be seen as essential to male and female being.[52]

Womanist theologian Karen Baker-Fletcher, writing on "Difference," says, "Womanist and feminist theology and ethics argue for positive, nonhierarchical, moral, ontological, and aesthetic valuations of differences among humankind and in all creation. They emphasize solidarity and mutuality among human beings of diverse races, ethnicities, cultures, genders, classes, and sexual preferences."[53] Surely the work of God's Spirit is a valuing of difference, of mutual recognition that seeks to counter the devaluation brought on by hierarchical dualism. If "taste" can be taken as a metaphor for our uniqueness and diversity, then the Spirit honors each embodied perspective even while revealing our commonality. We are bread broken, bread shared.

In promoting the notion of "partnership," Letty Russell reminds us that "women have been unequal partners for centuries."[54] This inequality has been transferred also to the three persons of the Trinity, for as feminist and womanist theologians seek to speak of God in feminine language, God's very self becomes differently valued. This is especially true of the Spirit. Elizabeth Johnson ponders possible reasons why "theological articulation about the Spirit has traditionally lagged considerably behind reflection on God unoriginate source of all and God incarnate."[55] She offers several cogent suggestions from the history of theology, concluding with the suggestion that it is precisely the Spirit's femaleness that allows her to be forgotten:

So powerful is the association of Spirit with the meaning evoked by these female images that in recent years the theory has grown that one of the key if unarticulated reasons for the tradition's forgetfulness of the Spirit lies precisely here, in the alliance between the idea of Spirit and the roles and persons of actual women marginalized in church and society.[56]

Sarah Coakley raises serious questions about attempts by male theologians, Yves Congar in particular, to make the Holy Spirit feminine. "At worst," she says, "a 'feminine' Spirit may become nothing much more than the soothing but undervalued adjunct to the drama of an all-male household."[57] Like other feminist and womanist theologians, Coakley seeks a wholeness in theology and in social reality; with Ruether, she believes that "the hierarchical patterns of male activity and female passivity" must be transcended.[58]

Tasting the Spirit

Identifying with those feminists and womanists who relish both difference and wholeness, I seek to employ and subvert, to trust and suspect, divine femininity, longing for a day when qualities of nurture and hospitality become male virtues also, and when women are seen as powerful and omniscient. I close with a story that says more about hospitality, redemption, sanctification, and feminine spirituality than any argument or doctrine could convey, Isak Dinesen's delicious tale, "Babette's Feast."[59]

The abstemious, puritanical sisters Martina and Philippa reluctantly welcome the alien exile, Babette, into their home. Formerly a great chef in Paris, Babette becomes the servant of the Danish sisters, aiding in their ministry to a group of devout believers founded by their father, serving them as "the dark Martha in the house of their two fair Marys." When she comes into some money, she begs the sisters to allow her to prepare a real French dinner for their father's disciples. Food and wine, quail and a live tortoise are shipped from France. The pious, contentious, and disapproving faithful are invited, vowing together to silently and ascetically partake of the sumptuous feast.

The story culminates in the anniversary dinner: The twelve "were sitting down to a meal, well, so had the people done at the wedding at Cana. And grace has chosen to manifest itself there, in the very wine, as fully as anywhere." As the disciples feasted, unaware of the meal's true value, they were transformed from squabbling neighbors to light-hearted friends. As the wine flowed, happy memories were renewed, spirits reborn. The twelfth guest, invited at the last moment, is so moved that he rises and speaks of the infinite grace of God, grace that "demands nothing from us but that we shall await it with confidence and acknowledge it in gratitude."

When the sisters realize that their maid was once a famous chef and that she had spent her fortune on the meal, they protest: "Dear Babette, you ought not to have given away all you had for our sake." "For your sake?" she replies. "No. For my own...I am a great artist." As Babette had turned the food in the Café Anglais into "a kind of love affair...in which one no longer distinguishes between bodily and spiritual appetite or satiety," so her meal had transformed the aged, pious disciples into loving children without their knowing it and despite their resistance.

Just so, the Spirit of God satisfies our hunger and sanctifies our tastes, subverting our desire to resist and our longing to universalize our own particularities. Dinesen's story is eucharistic, for food and wine transform, redeem, renew. Her redeemer is female, hardly domesticated, opening stifled senses to the sensuous, lavish grace of God, and welcoming the very strangers who once welcomed her.

Feeling, Fire, Fervor

Kindling Comfort

Growing up in California, firebuilding was hardly, if ever, a necessity. In fact, even firing up the furnace was a rarity. When I took a pastoral position in Scotland and occupied a Victorian flat owned by the kirk, my firebuilding skills took on a new urgency, for the marble mantelpiece with its small iron grate was the only source of heat in those drafty living quarters. Coal was delivered by two thoroughly Dickensian characters who stood at the bottom of the stairwell shouting, "cowl, cowl," and, finding me home, huffed their way up three flights, depositing the black lumps in a closet designed to hold them. I learned just how to twist sheets of newspaper into tight little sticks. I employed small white cubes called "firestarters." I foraged for kindling on the streets of Edinburgh and found that discarded fruit crates were easily broken up and ignited. If I packed the coals tightly just before I went to bed, a few dying embers might get the fire going again in the morning. Once the fire was burning and the coals became red hot, the room became cozy and comfortable, as long as the doors and windows were shut tight.

Parishioners would ask me how I liked the flat. "It's cold," I'd say in response. "Have you no gas fire?" they'd ask. "No, just a coal fire and an electric blanket." "Och, well, a coal fire's lovely now, isn't it?" came the reply. It gradually dawned on me that few, if any, of the natives built coal fires just to keep warm, but they remembered fondly a time in the distant past before their homes were fitted with proper heaters.

There is something cheery and comforting about a fire. The warmth of a crackling fire is particularly welcoming and welcome on a cold winter's day. As room temperature rises and the chill is defeated, one is invited to sit still, to relax, to stay put, to settle in. The atmosphere is most conducive to reading, to reflection, to shared conversation. Every so often the fire is stoked and the warmth sustained.

God's Spirit warms and comforts; God's Spirit burns and burnishes; God's Spirit lures and cajoles us as we seek to follow, as God seeks us out. Our passionate love for God burns as a flame within, a strange warming, a cheery welcome. From a place of comfort and belonging can we dream of risk and adventure. When we venture out, God's flaming presence guides us toward a place of rest and promise. Julian spoke of God as "everything which is good and comforting for our help...our clothing...that love which wraps and enfolds us, embraces us and guides us, surrounds us...so tender that [it] may never desert us."[1]

And yet the fiery flames of God's passionate Spirit are also discomforting, even dangerous at times. The fiery Spirit leads and guides us, warms and welcomes, but the fiery Spirit also refines and consumes, disarms and dislodges us. We begin to find that the sensuality of the Spirit is at once tame and wild, for wind and fire, earth and water, are as hazardous as they are healing.

As I stepped out onto my porch to retrieve the Sunday paper, I felt the dry wind moving off the mountains toward the sea. In Southern California such winds, Santa Anas, are common, but in the Bay Area the cool sea breezes normally flow inward. Looking up into the hills I saw a tiny column of smoke, left over, I assumed, from a small fire that had been contained the night before. An hour later, when I left for church, the sky was filled with smoke, the flames visible, growing, moving. As the day wore on, friends were leaving their homes behind, fleeing the firestorm. By the time it was over, nearly 4,000 homes were destroyed. Living just a few miles away, that Oakland hills fire was more than a news story, it was too close for comfort.[2]

In the aftermath of that fire, many things became clear. Home and hearth can be destroyed in an instant, an instant in which the relative importance of things and people quickly falls into place. The fire was a leveling that revealed the layers of classism: the hill homes covered by insurance, the apartment dwellers with no insurance, the domestic workers who lived in the flatlands and lost their livelihood when their employers' homes burned. Churches and relief agencies learned to work together. With the passing of time, the scarred, treeless hills were once again inhabited.

They say that fire is a natural part of the forest ecology, that every so often the undergrowth needs to be burned away, the populations thinned. Yet it is hard to sense any good in a destructive fire, except perhaps the lessons to be learned once it's all over. The fire that we kindle in our hearths and hearts can become a consuming, refining fire, at once inviting and injurious. Kindling both comfort and compassion is the shared work of human spirit and Holy Spirit.

Holy Fire

Images of fire in the Hebrew Bible tend to be more of the discomforting sort. There is clearly a punitive, adversarial aspect to fire. Fire is used in warfare to destroy one's enemies, and God is seen as using it to punish Israel's enemies (Josh. 6:24; 11:6–9; Judg. 12:1; 14:15; Neh. 1:3–17); God goes before Israel "as a devouring fire" (Deut. 9:3). The seventh plague, hail, thunder, and lightning (Ex. 9:23–24), is recounted in Psalm 18 as a paradigm of God's commanding and fiery power:

> With fiery breath and blazing nostrils
> God split open the heavens,
> coming down on dense clouds…
> with flaming clouds,
> with hail and coals of fire,
> the Lord almighty thundered from the heavens,
> aimed lightning bolts like arrows
> to rout the enemy. (Ps. 18:9–10, 13–15, *The Psalter*)

Fire represents God's wrath, consuming, burning, jealous, turned not only on Israel's enemies but at times on the wayward Israelites.

For instance, God's anger was kindled when the people complained, and "the fire of the LORD burned against them, and consumed some outlying parts of the camp. But the people cried out to Moses; and Moses prayed to the LORD, and the fire abated. So that place was called Taberah, because the fire of the LORD burned against them" (Num. 11:1–3).

In the poetic and prophetic books, fire is a figurative way of speaking about God's anger. "How long, O LORD? Will you hide yourself forever? How long will your wrath burn like fire?" (Ps. 89:46; cf. Ps. 79:5) God is seen as commanding all the forces of nature—earth, water, fire, and wind:

> Praise the LORD from the earth,
>   you sea monsters and all deeps,
> fire and hail, snow and frost,
>   stormy wind fulfilling his command! (Ps. 148:7–8)

Fire will be the means of judgment upon those who turn from God:

> For the LORD will come in fire,
>   and his chariots like the whirlwind,
> to pay back his anger in fury,
>   and his rebuke in flames of fire.
> For by fire will the LORD execute judgment,
>   and by his sword, on all flesh;
>   and those slain by the LORD shall be many. (Isa. 66:15–16)

Nahum and Lamentations both speak of God's fury being "poured out like fire" (Nah. 1:6; Lam. 2:4). Ezekiel is particularly fond of fiery imagery and speaks often of God's wrath, jealousy, and righteous indignation:

> I will pour out my indignation upon you,
>   with the fire of my wrath
>   I will blow upon you.
> I will deliver you into brutish hands,
>   those skillful to destroy.
> You shall be fuel for the fire,
>   your blood shall enter the earth;
> You shall be remembered no more,
>   for I the LORD have spoken. (Ezek. 21:31–32)

Such images are unsettling, discomforting, hard to ignore. Yet if we allow ourselves to feel only the kind and comforting warmth of the Spirit, repentance becomes unnecessary. God's righteous anger burns, to be sure, against injustice and idolatry, but the prophets speak also of a holy, purifying aspect to this divine fire. In Isaiah 6, the prophet's encounter with God is accompanied by fire and smoke; Isaiah's sinfulness is burned away by the glowing coal of God's holiness (Isa. 6:1–7). God's consuming fire has a refining quality. The prophet Jeremiah is "a tester and refiner" among God's people: "The bellows blow fiercely, the lead is consumed by the fire; in vain the refining goes on, for the wicked are not removed" (Jer. 6:29). Malachi extends this metaphor of refined metal:

> For he is like a refiner's fire and like fullers' soap; he will sit as a refiner and purifier of silver, and he will purify the descendants of Levi and refine them like gold and silver, until they present offerings to the LORD in righteousness. Then the offering of Judah and Jerusalem will be pleasing to the LORD as in the days of old and as in former years. (Mal. 3:2–4)

While the fire of God, especially God's burning wrath, is often a sign of divine/human enmity, fire can also be a mediating, reconciling presence. A smoking fire pot and a flaming torch pass between Abram and God, signifying God's covenant (Gen. 15:17–18). Offerings to God from cereal grain to passover lamb are parched and roasted by fire (Lev. 2:14; Ex. 12:8–9; 2 Chr. 35:13). Isaac carried the kindling for his father's supreme sacrifice (Gen. 22:6–7). The fire of sacrifice was viewed as pleasing to God and thus a means of atonement and reconciliation.[3]

Clearly, there are sacrifices that are not pleasing to God, fire that is unholy. Fire was used to melt gold for the golden calf and to destroy it (Ex. 32:20–24). Unholy fire offered by the sons of Aaron was met with divine fire (Lev. 10:1–2). The idolatry of foreign sacrifice was seen as illicit, an abomination. The historical writings repeatedly condemn the ungodly practice of child sacrifice, in which the sons and daughters of foreigners were sent through fiery flames (2 Kings 16:3;17:17, 31; 21:6; 23:10; 2 Chr. 28:3). Perhaps the most dramatic portrayal of holy fire is the story of Elijah at Mount Carmel, in which the God of Israel defeats the Baals with consuming flames (1 Kings

18:20–40). Idols forged with fire are destroyed by fire (Deut. 7:5–6; Isa. 44:9–20).

Holy fire kindles a right relationship with God; holy fire also represents the very presence of God. God appeared to Moses in the burning bush (Ex. 3:2) and in the fiery cloud on Mount Sinai (Ex. 19:18; 24:17). The deuteronomist summarizes these divine encounters (Deut. 4:11–36), offering words of warning: "So be careful not to forget the covenant that the LORD your God made with you, and not to make for yourselves an idol in the form of anything that the LORD your God has forbidden you. For the LORD your God is a devouring fire, a jealous God" (vv. 23–24). This fiery God guides the people with a pillar of cloud by day, of fire by night (Ex. 13:21–22; 14:24; Deut. 1:32–33; Neh. 9:12,19).

Glorious Presence

The presence of God is both awesome and intimate, for the fiery Spirit who burns forth in flame and smoke also makes a home among the people. Clearly God is emotionally engaged with humankind. God is jealous when we worship other gods; God is angry and hurt by betrayal, by stubborn and stiff-necked behavior, by injustice. This fiery fury expresses God's relational being, not an impassible, total otherness but God's utter engagement with us. The smoky cloud signified the place of divine/human meeting, of intercourse between the Israelites and their God.

The verb *shakhan* and the noun *mishkan* speak of God's dwelling, settling, abiding with the people of Israel. Throughout the wilderness wanderings, the smoky cloud of God's presence hung over the tabernacle, God's very abode. Exodus 25—30 describes this tabernacle (*mishkan*) at the center of the camp, God's habitation, the place where God's name dwells.[4] "I will dwell among the Israelites, and I will be their God. And they shall know that I am the LORD their God, who brought them out of the land of Egypt that I might dwell among them; I am the LORD their God" (Ex. 29:45–46).

This holy habitation, whether tabernacle, tent, or temple, was a home for God's glory, *kabod*—an honor, a richness, a weight. Moses encountered God's glory on Mount Sinai and in the tent of meeting (Ex. 34:29–35; 40:34–35). The same warm and weighty glory that caused Moses' face to shine filled Solomon's temple (2 Chr. 7:1–3). Ultimately, this glory resides with God's people: "Surely his salvation is at hand for those who fear him, that his glory may dwell in our land" (Ps. 85:9). God makes an abode, a sanctuary, on earth:

> I will make a covenant of peace with them; it shall be an everlasting covenant with them; and I will bless them and multiply them, and will set my sanctuary among them forevermore. My dwelling place shall be with them; and I will be their God, and they shall be my people. Then the nations shall know that I the LORD sanctify Israel, when my sanctuary is among them forevermore. (Ezek. 37:26–28)

The Holy One is at home on the mountaintop and in human hearts:

> For thus says the high and lofty one
> who inhabits eternity, whose name is Holy:
> I dwell in the high and holy place,
> and also with those who are contrite and humble in spirit,
> to revive the spirit of the humble,
> and to revive the heart of the contrite. (Isa. 57:15)

The glory of God is a felt presence, a weighty substance, a radiating warmth, filling, infusing human hearts and the sanctuary of creation itself. This glowing glory heartens and challenges, changes and chastens us; this sacred heat finds a form in earthen vessels, molded clay fired in holy kilns. The apostle Paul links the transforming glory of God with embodied existence, joining Moses and the tent of meeting with the Spirit and the clay jars in which she dwells. In a passage often interpreted in a supersessionist way,[5] Paul speaks of the glory of God's Spirit:

> Now the Lord is the Spirit, and where the Spirit of the Lord is, there is freedom. And all of us, with unveiled faces, seeing the glory of the Lord as though reflected in a mirror, are being transformed into the same image from one degree of glory to another; for this comes from the Lord, the Spirit.
> (2 Cor. 3:17–18)

Paul and other New Testament writers are often seen as reading the Holy Spirit out of the Hebrew Bible, as sensing the Spirit to be God's gift to the church. It should be clear by now that I find it as anti-Jewish to read the Spirit *out* of the Hebrew Bible as it is to read christology *into* it. The Spirit of the Lord *is* the Spirit of Jahweh. The indwelling glory of God, the *kabod,* the *shakhan,* finds a home in the earthen vessels of our bodies as surely as in tabernacle, temple, tent, or mountaintop. Paul is realistic about the limits, the heaviness of bodily existence:

> So we do not lose heart. Even though our outer nature is wasting away, our inner nature is being renewed day by day. For this slight momentary affliction is preparing us for an eternal weight of glory beyond all measure, because we look not at what can be seen but at what cannot be seen; for what can be seen is temporary, but what cannot be seen is eternal. (2 Cor. 4:16–18)

Again, Paul's eschatological certitude, his conviction that the Parousia was imminent, lures him into the future, a future in which there will be bodies and tents and dwellings (2 Cor. 5:1–5). Like other Pauline passages, this one is prone to dualistic interpretation. Paul does sound dualistic in terms of time and eternity, of visible and invisible, of inner and outer, but he is realistic about embodiment; while this body is temporal and limited, God's Spirit makes a home here and is at work transforming, molding, refining.

Baptism by Fire

Christian theology has sometimes taught that the God of the New Testament is kinder and gentler than the wrathful God of the Hebrew Bible. Yet the fiery presence of God's Spirit persists in Christian scripture as well. John the Baptist said, "I baptize you with water; but one who is more powerful than I is coming; I am not worthy to untie the thong of his sandals. He will baptize you with the Holy Spirit and fire" (Lk. 3:16; cf. Mt. 3:11–12; Mk. 1:7–8). The Holy Spirit appeared in tongues of flame at Pentecost (Acts 2:3).

Apocalyptic literature also bears witness to the fire of God (Mt. 18:8; 25:41; Lk. 12:49). In John's vision, reminiscent of prophetic visions, the Son of Man has eyes "like a flame of fire...feet like burnished bronze, refined as in a furnace" (Rev. 1:14–15). In the end, a burning lake of fire consumes the damned (Rev. 20:10; 21:8). The refining power of fire is here also, especially for believers who go through trials as tests of their sincerity (1 Pet. 4:12). Fruitless branches, weeds, and chaff are burned (Mt. 3:12; Jn. 15:6). God is a consuming fire, one who can protect and destroy (Heb. 12:29).

Fiery images can be holy or unholy in the Christian Testament as in the Hebrew. Passions burn, including sinful passions. The hearts of Jesus' friends on the Road to Emmaus burned within them as he opened to them the Scriptures (Lk. 24:32). James likens the tongue to fire, a fire that can be tame or wild, uttering blessing or curse (Jas. 3:5–10). Fleshly passions can burn out of control (1 Cor. 7:9).

Yet this fiery, passionate God also dwells within, making a tabernacle with mortals, comforting, caring (Rev. 21:3–4). The Spirit makes a home in the temples of our bodies, kindling holy compassion and truth. The Paraclete, the Comforter, the Helper, the Spirit of Truth is also advocate, counselor, exhorter (Jn. 14:16–17, 26), abiding with us, teaching us God's ways.

Shekhinah/Spirit

With the destruction of the Jerusalem temple in 70 C.E., Jewish beliefs about the presence of God were reconstructed. Hebrew worship moved from temple to home to synagogue, where groups of families observed together. Feasts like Passover and Sukkoth were celebrated in homes and family groups rather than in Jerusalem. About this time, rabbinic tradition began to speak of the *Shekhinah*, the presence, the dwelling of God, the intimate habitation of God with God's people.[6] In typical rabbinic fashion, teachings about Shekhinah evolved through argument, midrash, and Talmud. Some believed Shekhinah to be in exile with God's people (*Shekhinta b'Galuta*); others believed Shekhinah to be confined in the stones of the temple or to the halakhic study of the Torah (*tsimtsum ha-Shekhinah*); still others used the terms *Shekhinah* and *Holy Spirit* interchangeably.[7]

Though Shekhinah is a rabbinic rather than a biblical word, it is rooted in *shakhan* and *mishkhan*. Shekhinah is read back into Hebrew scripture to name God's presence in the burning bush, on Sinai, in the pillar of fire and cloud, and with, within, and among God's people.[8] Lodahl and others note that Shekhinah is the intimate, friendly, immanent neighborliness of God, the God who is with us and within us, "God's comforting and sustaining presence"; he summarizes: "For the rabbis, both 'the Holy Spirit' and 'the Shekhinah' were terms which referred to God's presence, experienced most fully in the communal encounter with the divine address and command of the sacred text, and in faithful response to the word that is heard."[9]

In the Middle Ages, Jewish mysticism flourished, as did Christian. The Kabbalists took this notion of Shekhinah much further than many rabbis would have dreamed. In Kabbalah, God's names, or attributes, are associated with ten *sefirot*—"lights" that comprise the life of God.[10] Shekhinah, or Presence, is the tenth or "lowest" of the sefirot and conveys God's nearness to the world. Shekhinah is female, and according to the Kabbalists, with Binah (understanding, womb) represents the feminine dimension of God's being. The sefirot were also seen as representing God's body, the head, the arms, the torso; Shekhinah was associated with the female genitalia, the "opening to the divine."[11]

The later Kabbalists developed a kind of creation, fall, and redemption myth that speaks of the immanence of divine fire and of humanity's part in the restoration of creation. The sixteenth-century teacher Isaac Luria sought to reinterpret rabbinic notions of creation by pondering the idea of *tsimtsum,* divine confinement or withdrawal.[12] Scholem calls this "one of the most amazing and far-reaching conceptions ever put forward in the whole history of Kabbalism." Rather than the emanation of the Neoplatonists, creation was a retreat, a shrinkage. According to Scholem,

> the existence of the universe is made possible by a process of shrinkage in God…God was compelled to make room for the world by, as it were, abandoning a region within Himself, a kind of mystical primordial space from which He withdrew in order to return to it in the act of creation and revelation.[13]

Along with *tsimtsum,* Luria taught *shevirath,* the breaking of the vessels, and *tikkun,* the mending of creation. Both divine grace and divine judgment abide in the vessels of creation; eventually creation is fractured, shattered by the tension between evil and holiness.[14] The fire of creation is trapped as sparks in the shards of broken pottery that make up creation. According to Matt, "the human task is to liberate, or raise, these sparks, to restore them to divinity."[15] The process of "raising the sparks" is known as *tikkun,* or mending. Humanity now has a part not only in the restoration of creation but in the restoration of God's very being. Matt quotes the Kabbalist, Israel Sarug:

When the shards descended to the bottom of the world of actualization, they were transformed into the four elements—fire, air, water, and earth—from which evolved the stages of mineral, vegetable, animal, and human. When these materialized, some of the sparks remained hidden within the varieties of existence. You should aim to raise those sparks hidden throughout the world, elevating them to holiness by the power of your soul.[16]

"Raising the sparks," or *tikkun,* has become a call to holy living, an affirmation of the intimate connection between God's Spirit and creation, between indwelt vessels and divine wholeness.

A question arises as to whether the Shekhinah, the indwelling presence of God, is, indeed, the very Spirit of God. Lodahl speaks of Shekhinah/Spirit as a trope "for God's own active nearness to creation, to humanity, and particularly to Israel."[17] He wants to question the exclusivity of much Christian pneumatology: "By beginning Trinitarian reflection with the Spirit as God's active, alluring presence in creation, and as the animating call to human beings to grow in the Creator's image of response-ability, there is ground for opposition to much of traditional Christianity's triumphalistic exclusivisim."[18] This line of thought resonates with that of Elizabeth Johnson, who begins her Trinitarian reflection with Spirit-Sophia, "God's ongoing transcending engagement with the world."[19] God's fiery Spirit abides with us as both judgment and grace, kindling in us holiness and kindness, calling us to "raise the sparks" and participate in the mending of creation.

Liturgical Fire

Just as Jewish worship went "home" following the destruction of the temple, so early Christian worship was a domestic phenomenon. In fact, since the earliest Christians still viewed themselves as Jews, their worship drew from Jewish practice. Though lamps were a practical necessity, we know that Jewish worship, in temple and synagogue, involved lampstands and menorahs. While the precise influences of Jewish worship on Christian are unclear, there are early references to liturgical lamps, which suggest that the burning lamps had some meaning in worship beyond their practical use.[20] Though New Testament and early patristic references are inconclusive, by the fourth century we have a number of references to the use of lamps and candles in Christian worship. The *Acts of Munatus Felix* (303 C.E.) mentions a number of vessels found in a house-church, including "seven short bronze candlesticks with their candles, [and] eleven bronze lamps with their chains."[21]

In the Constantinian era, practices that had been viewed as pagan were sacralized and made Christian, including the liturgical use of lamps, incense, and fire.[22] During this time the celebration of the Paschal Vigil, with its service of light, was first observed. We know from the writings of Egeria that the vigil was practiced in Jerusalem in the fifth century.[23] The Easter Vigil begins on Easter Eve with the lighting of the New Fire from which the paschal candle is ignited, a tradition thought to have originated in Ireland.[24] In some places the hearth fires of believers were extinguished on Maundy Thursday, dramatizing the cessation of both light and warmth in the betrayal and death of Jesus. The New Fire was kindled in secret, in Jerusalem within the Anastasis, and the service of light began. From the paschal candle all present lit their tapers singing the *Exultet:* "Rejoice!…This is the night when the pillar of fire destroyed the darkness of sin."[25] In certain places, the burning tapers were taken home and used to rekindle the home fires.[26]

The extinguishing of the fire during the time of Christ's death and burial dramatizes the apparent absence of God's Spirit between the crucifixion and resurrection. Though Jesus experienced God as forsaking him on the cross, Moltmann maintains that "On Golgotha the Spirit suffers the suffering and death of the Son, without dying with him."[27] With the psalmist, we affirm the presence of the Spirit even in darkest Sheol (Ps. 139:8). Rather than abandonment or absence, the Shekhinah/Spirit is in exile as the temple of Christ's body is destroyed. The rekindling of the fire is an act of faith, a sign of the Spirit's return, an emblem of God's promise not to forsake us.

Heartfelt Spirituality

As we have seen, a wide variety of sensual imagery is typical of mystical visions, and mystics often describe their bodily sensations during these visions. Bright light, calming and prophetic voices, scenes of the passion, erotic desire, hunger, thirst, the fragrance of flowers, and the odor of decay are all found in the writings of the mystics.

It should come as no surprise that the medieval mystics often employed fiery images to speak of the presence of the Spirit and union with God. Revelation came to Hildegard in the form of fiery flames:

"Heaven was opened and a fiery light of exceeding brilliance came and permeated my whole brain, and inflamed my whole heart and my whole breast, not like a burning but like a warming flame, as the sun warms anything its rays touch."[28] Hildegard's vision of the Trinity was like a bright light "blazing with a gentle glowing fire."[29] "As the flame of a fire has three qualities," Hildegard writes, "brilliant light and red power and fiery heat...so the Three Persons must be understood in the Unity of the Divinity."[30]

The beguine Mechtild of Magdeburg is typical of the women mystics in her use of sensual images and in their variety. The beguines were women who chose to live in religious community but not under any official rule. This movement flourished in the thirteenth century but by 1318 was considered heretical; many beguines and beghards (their male counterparts) were persecuted or forced to join approved orders.[31] Beguine spirituality found its home in the Rhineland and the Low Countries, and the convent of Helfta, where Mechtild ultimately found refuge, was an important center.

Mechtild wrote seven books, which recorded her spiritual experiences, daily "greetings" from the Holy Spirit. These seven books, written between 1250 and 1270, make up *The Flowing Light of the Godhead*. In Mechtild's writings, the body and soul form an "uneasy partnership."[32] Though there is an urge to transcend the limitations of sensate, somatic existence, Mechtild recognizes the connections between the real feelings of her bodily life and her spiritual aspirations. Though many sensual images typify her work, the intercourse between human heart and divine heart is central to Mechtild's spiritual reflection. In union with God,

...eye reflects eye
...spirit flows in spirit
...hand touches hand
...mouth speaks to mouth
...heart greets heart. (IV.14)

Mechtild employs powerful sensual language, describing Jesus' wounds and Mary's breasts as sources of succor:

Both his wounds and her breasts were open
The wounds poured forth
The breasts flowed
The soul was invigorated and completely restored

As he poured the sparkling red wine
Into her red mouth. (I.22)

The Flowing Light is also replete with nuptial imagery, the visionary often referring to herself as the Bride and employing the genres of
courtly love.[33] All the senses, including sound, are evoked as well:
"The Godhead rings/Humanity sings/The Holy Spirit plucks the harp
of the heavens/So that all strings resound/They are strung in love" (II.3).

Heartfelt longing and fiery passion go together; burning warmth
and heavenly love are qualities of the divine indwelling. Though fiery
images burn throughout the text, an extended vision of divine fire is
laid out in Book VI, chapter 29. God is an eternal fire; the angels and
the saints are sparks and "bright flickerings." "The everlasting coals
of the fire are all the blessed here on earth who are on fire with heavenly love and shine with good example." The fire's reign is yet to
come, a forging of holy vessels. Earthly desires are likened to smoke,
the future judgment to the fire's bitterness. For believers, God's fire is
comforting, "the delightful pleasure that our soul receives inwardly
from God through the warmth of the divine fire."

Reforming Pietism

In her book, audaciously titled *A History of God*, former nun Karen
Armstrong concludes her chapter on mysticism with these words: "In
England, Germany and the Lowlands, which had produced such distinguished mystics, the Protestant Reformers of the sixteenth century
decried this unbiblical spirituality...As a result of the Reformation,
Europe began to see God in still more rationalistic terms."[34] Such
sweeping generalizations about the sixteenth-century reforms betray
certain deeply held misconceptions about the origins of Protestantism and the spirituality of the Reformers. Though there was certainly
a turn to rationalism after the sixteenth century, this can hardly be
seen as a purely Protestant phenomenon; and though the Reformers
decried much that they found unbiblical, spirituality, even that of the
mystics, was greatly appreciated by Luther and Calvin, in particular.

While it may be true that later developments in Lutheran and
Reformed theology have obscured the spirituality of the Reformers,
their deep appreciation for mystical and spiritual writers is well-
documented. In a work that details mystical influences on Luther,
Bengt Hoffman writes, "Martin Luther's faith-consciousness was

significantly molded by mystical experience, and...Western dependence on rationalism has obscured or eclipsed this mystical light."[35] Luther had a great appreciation for Johannes Tauler and is credited with bringing to publication the *Theologia Germanica*, an anonymous work by a German mystic.

Calvin's *Institutes of the Christian Religion* were written with the express purpose of promoting piety, which Calvin defined as "that reverence joined with love of God which the knowledge of his benefits induces" (I.ii.1).[36] In a section on the biblical titles for the Holy Spirit (III.i.3), Calvin writes, "persistently boiling away and burning up our vicious and inordinate desires, he enflames our hearts with the love of God and with zealous devotion. From this effect upon us he is also justly called 'fire' [Lk. 3:16]."[37] Like Luther, Calvin's writings show the influence of a number of mystical writers, including Jean Gerson and Bernard of Clairvaux.[38]

Perhaps because these Reformers emphasized understanding and valued scholarship, Protestant theology, like Catholic theology, was worked out more often in scholastic and doctrinal modes than in spiritual and mystical texts. By the time of the Enlightenment, Protestant dogmaticians had out-systematized the very medieval scholastics Calvin and Luther had sought to reform. Both Protestant scholasticism and the religion of reason, typified by the Deists, seemed, to many believers, utterly devoid of piety.

The Pietists, as they were called, reacted to the rationalism of both orthodoxy and Deism by appealing to religious experience, an emphasis on heartfelt knowing. Count von Zinzendorf, leader of the Moravians, the spiritual descendants of Jan Hus, writes of faithful knowing: "One knows in his innermost person with whom he deals. One knows him from head to foot, in heart and body...when one has thought and felt this long enough...then one takes out one truth after other, presents it and demonstrates it with reasons grounded deep within oneself, which grasp the hearers' hearts."[39] Zinzendorf, like other Pietists, often speaks of feeling, including a powerful apprehension of Christ's bodily suffering, *Jesum in Carne*, in the flesh, as Augustine put it.[40]

John Wesley was deeply influenced by the spirituality of the Moravians. In a pivotal entry from his *Journal*, Wesley speaks of studying Luther with the British Moravian, Peter Böhler: "About a quarter before nine, while he was describing the change which God works in the heart through faith in Christ, I felt my heart strangely warmed. I felt I did trust in Christ, Christ alone, for salvation; and an assurance was given me that He had taken away my sins, even mine, and saved me from the law of sin and death."[41] Soon after this experience, Wesley went to Germany to learn from the Moravians. It is no surprise that Schleiermacher, who made the notion of feeling, *Gefühl*, central to his theology, was raised a Moravian as well.[42]

Unholy Fire

Even as holy fire burned in the hearts of the pious, unholy fires burned throughout Christendom. Just as the idolatrous, the false prophets, had displeased the fiery God of Israel with their sacrifices, so also, in the name of Christ, the guardians of the orthodoxy burned heretics and witches. Heresy trials and witch hunts raged out of control and crossed all political and ecclesiastical boundaries. Heretics were viewed as a threat from earliest Christianity, but beginning in the twelfth century, the papacy established ecclesiastical courts to preserve the true faith. Not only the books but the bodies of many heretics were burned. The Inquisition raged most furiously at the end of the fifteenth century in Spain, when Queen Isabella banished Jews and Moors from her realm. While Protestants were targets of the Inquisition in the sixteenth century, the unholy fires burned also in lands where the Reformation had taken hold.

We have already noted that beguines were suspect, for they lived without an official Rule; many were executed, from Aleydis in 1236 to Margrete Porete in 1310. As late as 1421, the Archbishop of Cologne was ordered "to search out and destroy any small convents of persons living under the cloak of religion without a definite Rule."[43] In 1414 the Council of Constance condemned the Bohemian reformer Jan Hus, in part, for suggesting that communion should be received in both kinds by the faithful. He was burned at the stake in 1415. The body of John Wycliffe was removed from holy ground. We know that Wycliffe's followers in England, the Lollards, were burned if found to be in possession of English Bibles. In 1486 the *Malleus Maleficarum* was published by the German Inquisition, with its vicious attacks on women, who were seen to be more prone to witchcraft than men because of their created defects and their carnal nature: "All witchcraft comes from carnal lust, which is in women insatiable."[44]

Unholy fire was not limited to the Inquisition of the Roman Church; Protestants also burned heretics, witches, and the occasional bishop. Michael Servetus was arrested by the Inquisition in France for his anti-Trinitarian and Anabaptist views but escaped to Protestant Geneva, where Calvin had him arrested. The civil authorities burned Servetus alive, but with the aid of testimony from Calvin and other Protestant pastors.[45] In response to the burning of Scottish reformer, George Wishart, in St. Andrews in 1546, Cardinal Beaton was brutally murdered in the same spot by Wishart's sympathizers. While we remember the exploits of Bloody Mary toward Protestants in Tudor England, our memory is more vague regarding the execution of Roman Catholics in the Elizabethan era.[46]

Anne Llewellyn Barstow, in *Witchcraze,* notes the lack of gender analysis in recent research on the European witch hunts, as well as the severity of their violence and its sexual nature.[47] Though most researchers acknowledge the preponderance of female victims, misogyny is seldom mentioned as a cause. Barstow, by bringing a feminist critique to the research and by sharing with her readers the lurid details of the executions, demonstrates the deep hatred for women and the widespread campaign of fear enacted throughout Christendom— among Protestants and Catholics alike. The witchcraze was a pogrom of the elite and powerful against witchcraft, which was seen as part of a "folk culture," an attack, says Llewellyn, "on basic customs and values of the people."[48] Women who did not have familial protection, who were economically marginalized, yet whose power was feared, became the targets of the witch hunters.

Barstow tells the story of Anna Pappenheimer, who was imprisoned, tortured, and stripped, her breasts cut off and "forced into her mouth and…the mouths of her two grown sons," then burned alive as a crowd of vested clergy watched, singing a hymn, with church bells pealing.[49]

> Anna's body was a human sacrifice to the Christian God…Society did not invest her flesh with any saving power, nor her ashes, even after they had been purified in the flames…this was not a ritual with the power of atonement; it was a ritual of revenge. Its power over contemporaries lay in the amount of suffering it caused, in the amount of fear it generated; it did not heal. In fact it was entirely destructive, unless, that is, one considers its teaching function to be a positive one. As a didactic device, the ritual executions of witches succeeded superbly.[50]

The fires of the witchcraze were unholy fires, like the fires of the Shoah and those that burn crosses and churches even today; they are the fires of hate and fear, an abomination to a holy and loving God, a betrayal of the very Spirit that sustains and purifies martyrs in every age.

Pentecostal Fire

The fiery Spirit of God, the Spirit that inflamed the passions of prophets and apostles, cannot be tamed, nor can her ardor be controlled or contained—even by those who claim to be guarding the church's purity and holiness. Those of us who see ourselves as part of the mainstream certainly do not have a corner on the Spirit's power or holiness. In fact, it would seem that the fire of the Spirit often burns most fervently in the hearts of those who appear a bit eccentric to the centrists. This is not to say that witches are filled with the Spirit or that moderate mainliners always quench her fiery passion. We have seen what great harm has been done in the name of holiness, and we have sensed the Spirit's power made manifest in some unexpected people and places.

As a mainline Protestant, one whose ministry is among a people sometimes referred to as God's "frozen chosen," I admit that Pentecostal fire makes me a bit uncomfortable at times. However, a quick survey of the growth of Pentecostalism worldwide would suggest it is, indeed, spreading "like wildfire." Michael Welker calls the Charismatic movement, by which he means the growth of both Pentecostal churches and charismatic renewal movements within established denominations, "the fastest growing religious movement of our time...the largest religious movement in history, period."[51]

Most trace the beginnings of the modern Pentecostal movement to events in the U.S. early in this century. Nancy Hardesty, in a chapter on "Evangelical Women," tells of Charles Fox Parham's ministry at Bethel College in Topeka, Kansas, where a student, Agnes Osman, spoke in tongues at a service on New Year's Day, 1901.[52] African American students of Parham preached and the Spirit's gifts were manifest at a Holiness church on Azusa Street in Los Angeles a few years later, a site that has been viewed as "ground zero" for the spread of global Pentecostalism.[53] Bryan Wilson traces the beginnings of the Charismatic Renewal to an Episcopal church in Van Nuys, California, in 1958, a movement of the Spirit, accompanied often by healing, prophecy, and glossolalia, within Catholic, Orthodox, and Reformation churches, first in the U.S., then worldwide.[54]

It is clear that women were deeply involved in kindling the fires of Pentecostalism. Nancy Hardesty tells of Florence Crawford, who founded the Pentecostal Apostolic Faith movement; of Alma White, founder of the Pillar of Fire church; of Aimee Semple McPherson, founder of the International Church of the Foursquare Gospel; and of an early radio and television healer-evangelist, Kathryn Kuhlman.[55] Hardesty also describes the "eclipse" of women in the Holiness and Pentecostal movements during the 1940s and 1950s. The authors of *Clergy Women: An Uphill Calling* attribute this eclipse to the institutionalizing process within these "Spirit-Centered" denominations; "The Spirit," they write, "was tamed by institutional practice and denominational assumptions about the nature of the church."[56]

Despite our best efforts, the fire of God's Spirit cannot be contained or tamed. It is the essence of this Spirit, who makes an abode in human hearts, to express herself in a wild diversity of *charismata*, yet to remain one Spirit. Jürgen Moltmann acknowledges the radical particularity of life: "Life is always specific, never general. Life is everywhere different, never the same. It is female or male, young or old, handicapped or non-handicapped, Jewish or Gentile, white or black, and so forth."[57] In a discussion of glossolalia, Welker uses the term *polyconcretism* to describe this particularity and the variety of individual concretions of the Spirit: "Like mystical 'experience' or modern ego-consciousness, speaking in tongues is a form that can be used and employed *either* in a manner that individuates *or* in a manner that makes connection, *either* in a manner that brings about disintegration *or* in a manner that fosters solidarity."[58] Unity in the Spirit is kindled not by universalizing our particularities but in the untamed but mystical communion of discrete, concrete *charismata*.

Ecumenical Spirit

Perhaps nowhere is this wild diversity, this "polyconcretism," made manifest as it is in the *oikoumene*, the global household of faith. The radical extremes of the Spirit's activity were drawn in bold relief at the Canberra Assembly of the World Council of Churches in 1991, a gathering around the theme "Come Holy Spirit." The most memorable and the most provocative presentation of that Assembly was an address by Chung Hyun Kyung, a Korean theologian who entered dancing to the beat of drums and who, after invoking the suffering spirits of history—from Hagar, to Joan of Arc, to those killed in the gas chambers and by atomic bombs—set fire to the paper from which she read.

It is no surprise that her words rattled the guardians of the orthodoxy, for she kindled her theology, in part, from traditional Korean religion, naming the sins of the Christian tradition and claiming that the Spirit's fire burns even in spirits neither Christian nor human. Her ancestors' spirits, their presence, and their cries she called "icons of the Holy Spirit—tangible and visible to us. Because of them, we can feel, touch and taste the concrete bodily historical presence of the Holy Spirit in our midst."[59] Chung called for metanoia, for repentance from anthropocentrism to life-centrism, from dualism to interconnection, from the culture of death to the culture of life.

Chung's litany of spirits made present the fires of hate that have burned throughout human history and too often in the name of religious faith. Unholy fires burn still, racist fires, misogynist fires, fires of ethnic cleansing, of Protestant-Catholic "troubles," of heterosexist fears, with new names added to the litany each day. An article previewing the Eighth Assembly of the World Council in Harare, Zimbabwe, is accompanied by excerpts from "Living Letters," telling of the oppression of women in South India, Lesotho, Argentina, Britain, Zambia, Myanmar, the U.S., Korea, Italy.[60]

Chung spoke in her 1991 address of the *Han*-ridden spirits, spirits fraught with anger, resentment, bitterness, and grief. While these feelings, when mixed with hate and fear, result in the kindling of unholy fire, Chung calls them "the raw energy for struggle for liberation."[61] We are reminded of the holy anger of God, bitter, grieving over injustice, idolatry, and betrayal. Righteous indignation, the feelings of *Han* mixed with love and justice, is a holy fire, too often quenched, especially when it burns in the hearts of passionate women. Rather than quiet submission, civility, and meekness, perhaps holy passion and righteous anger are the true signs of godly, Spirit-filled womanhood.[62]

The immense challenge of fervent, fiery, passionate, compassionate spirituality lies before us. How do we allow righteous indignation to burn, even to consume and refine, without becoming destructive? Moreover, where is the distinction between righteous anger and hate-filled fire? Here is where the holiness of God's Spirit holds sway, the holiness that fills us, dwells within us, but that is, nonetheless, distinct from us. This Spirit calls us to repentance, even as she judges our enemies; this same Spirit affirms us and comforts us, even while loving those we find hateful.

Remember the lake of fire, the holy wrath of God. Remember the kindling comfort of God, the welcoming warmth within. Just so, judgment and grace, mercy and justice are intertwined in the holiness, the wholeness of the Spirit's fire. "Without judgment," writes Marjorie Suchocki, "there is no justice."[63] All of us will ultimately comprehend the pain we have caused others, according to Suchocki; we will know as we are known. The perpetrator of suffering "will know her [i.e., the victim's] pain along with God's judgment of what might have been...he will experience God's feeling of her as a judgment of wrath against himself for what might have been."[64] The Comforter, even the Spirit of Truth, will remain both truthful and comforting; the Refiner's Fire, the Shekhinah, dwells with us, mercifully, and in holiness.

Aroma, Odor, Adoration

Smelly Memories

"Smells spur memories," writes Diane Ackerman, "but they also rouse our dozy senses, pamper and indulge us, help define our self-image, stir the cauldron of our seductiveness, warn us of danger, lead us into temptation, fan our religious fervor, accompany us to heaven."[1] Certain smells evoke childhood memories vividly. The smell of cigar smoke, stale or fresh, never fails to remind me of my maternal grandmother, Alice. No, grandma didn't smoke cigars, but my grandfather did, and so did Alice's second husband, who became a kind of step-grandfather to us after Papa Button died. The fragrance of the succulent iceplant reminds me of the walk up and down the steep hill to the beach where Alice lived. The smell of sea salt mixed with suntan lotion can take me back to those sunny, summer days.

Memories of my father's parents are evoked by the combined smell of coffee and cantaloupe, with or without bacon. If I close my eyes, I am eight years old, seated at the long table in their Hollywood home, eating breakfast with a varied collection of relatives. Certain smells always remind me of Southern California—smog laced with eucalyptus, jacaranda, chaparral; other combinations take me back to Scotland—new-mown grass with a hint of lavender, the stony mustiness of the cathedral. I can remember the smells of other people's houses, whereas ours always seemed neutral in terms of scent. It seems perfectly sensible to me that we can smell the scents and odors of others but are almost totally unaware of our own unique aroma.

God's Spirit is sensitive enough to recognize the subtle nuances, the peculiar aroma that each creature bears. Spiritual sensitivity enables us to sniff out the uniqueness of others and thereby to become aware of our own aromatic perspective. As the Spirit can discern an infinite array of scents, fair and foul, so she enables us to distinguish between the aromas of life and death. Through prayer we are linked with the communion of saints, as surely as their memories are evoked by their fragrance.

Diane Ackerman reminds us that animals have much more highly sensitive olfactory organs than do humans. That explains why my cats sniff at me jealously when I've petted someone else's cat or dog or why they sometimes like to sleep on my dirty laundry. Research suggests that evolution has adapted us to the fact that we humans no longer use our sense of smell for survival and so have fewer smell cells than our ancient ancestors or than our animal friends. Yet our sense of smell is keener than we imagine and more often aroused than consciousness allows, and we still find ways of marking our turf, of leaving our scent behind as we go.

When I tell people that my father is in the flavor and fragrance business, I often get a quizzical look at first, then the dawn of recognition. Of course, foods have flavors, even colors, added to them, but the idea that there are special smells added to the products we buy, including food, has only recently come to our awareness. Even so-called fragrance-free items have masking agents that give off a neutral aroma. My father always thought I had a pretty good nose and would sometimes test his samples on me. I remember the little brown bottles with their typed labels—"vanilla bean," "berry," "citrus," "new car," "leather," "lavender." Taste is a combination of color, flavor, odor. The subliminal power of smell is a keen marketing tool. Of all the fragrances my father sold, "cat odorant" was the most lucrative, a combination of smells that, when mixed with diatomaceous earth, would attract the cat to the box, mask the unpleasant odors, and smell fresh to the human cat lover's nose.

Diane Ackerman reminds us of the difficulty in finding words to describe all the subtleties of smell. Most often we describe smells in terms of something else—it smells like pine trees, like orange blossoms, like a cow barn. While we have words for all the colors in the rainbow, "the lavenders, mauves, fuchsias, plums, and lilacs—who will name the tones and tints of a smell?" Ackerman asks. A deeper sense of metaphor is awakened, for metaphors describe the indescribable by means of the familiar. The mystery of smell is itself a metaphor for the mystery of the divine: "Smells move us so profoundly, in part, because we cannot utter their names. In a world sayable and lush where marvels offer themselves up readily for verbal dissection, smells are often right on the tip of our tongues—but no closer—and it gives them a kind of magical distance, a mystery, a power without a name, a sacredness."[2]

So, too, God's Spirit is unsayable in the end, mysteriously elusive though close as the air that flows through our nostrils. The Spirit's very ubiquity enables us, as Spirit-filled creatures, to ponder the otherness and the commonality that lie between us and the rest of the created order. This ever-present breath of life helps us to discern and decide between goods and evils, between thoughts and words and actions that nurture health and wellness and those that deal in death and violence. Moreover, this indwelling Spirit enables a communication of idioms between human and divine, the incense of prayer.

Scriptural Scents

The priestly portions of Torah are thick with the scent of incense and oil, of spice and smoke. Exodus 25—30 and 35—40 offer extensive descriptions of the tabernacle where the worship of God took place; these instructions are further elaborated in Leviticus and Numbers and given narrative form in Chronicles, Kings, and Samuel. The sense of smell is aroused in at least three ways: by the fragrant oil of anointing, which is used to set apart both people and things to a holy purpose; by the smoke of sacrifice, which is a "pleasing odor" for God's nostrils; and by the spicy scent of incense, which rises toward God as prayer.

People, places, and things were made holy by the practice of cultic worship, by being drenched in the smells of sacrifice, praise, and prayer. Exodus 30 tells how the holy oil (*mishchah*) is to be blended, with myrrh, cinnamon, cane, cassia, and olive oil (vv. 23–24). Aaron and his sons are anointed to the priesthood in much the same way as kings were anointed to govern the people, with the consecration of this holy oil smeared on the head (v. 30; cf. 29:7; Lev. 8:10–13). The Aaronic priests were actually referred to as "anointed" and expected to practice holiness in all their doings, as were the Levites. Not only were priests anointed and vested, but the holy oil was used to consecrate the furnishings of tabernacle and temple (30:26–29). This holy oil was blended specially for worship by perfumers, and its use for profane purposes was forbidden (vv. 25, 32).

The priests and Levites of Israel were called to "minister to God":

> But as for us, the Lord is our God, and we have not abandoned him. We have priests ministering to the Lord who are descendants of Aaron, and Levites for their service. They offer to the Lord every morning and every evening burnt offerings and fragrant incense, set out the rows of bread on the table of pure gold, and care for the golden lampstand so that its lamps may burn every evening; for we keep the charge of the Lord our God, but you have abandoned him.
> (2 Chr. 13:10–11)

They were called to offer sacrifices of various kinds, grain and cereal, bird and beast, for the well-being and atonement of the people of Israel. The smoke of these sacrifices is called a "pleasing odor" to God (Ex. 29:18), in fact the term *re'ach*, which is related to *ruach*, becomes a synonym for sacrifice, even the illicit and unholy sacrifices of idolatry (Ezek. 6:13; 16:19; 20:28), pleasing, presumably, to some foreign god. Scripture suggests that God desires such sacrifice, delights in it, welcomes it, breathes it in. Right relationship with God depended on the faithful practice of the priests on behalf of the people.

Not only the smoke of sacrifice but the sweet smell of incense (*qatar*) was offered to God. Instructions for the blending of this incense and for its use were very specific (Ex. 30:34–38; Lev. 16:12). Incense was among the holy things, for the exclusive use of the priests (Ex. 30:7, 8; 1 Sam. 2:28). Incense signified prayer: "Let my prayer be counted as incense before you, and the lifting up of my hands as an evening sacrifice," writes the psalmist (Ps. 141:2). Offerings of incense alone were not enough to ensure holiness; holy living was to be part of the service of God:

Bringing offerings is futile;
incense is an abomination to me...
learn to do good; seek justice,
rescue the oppressed, defend the orphan,
plead for the widow. (Isa. 1:13, 17)

Proper priestly offerings were, in a very real way, the offerings of the people. In Exodus 25:1–9 (cf. 35:4–9), a list of goods is given which the people are to contribute for the building and maintenance of the tabernacle. The Israelites are asked to give of their riches, including valuable commodities like oil and spices, for the worship of God. It is clear that various kinds of fragrant oil and spices were considered signs of wealth and luxury and therefore rich gifts when offered for the worship of Yahweh. When the Queen of Sheba visited Solomon, she brought an abundance of spices along with all kinds of lavish gifts, and these spices became part of the extravagant worship in Solomon's temple (1 Kings 10:2, 10, 25; 2 Chr. 9:1, 9, 14). Hezekiah's treasure stores also included an abundance of spices (2 Kings 20:13; Isa. 39:2; cf. 2 Chr. 32:27).

Diane Ackerman calls the Song of Songs the most "smell-drenched" book in all the Bible, and indeed the love poem is dripping with all kinds of sensory stimulation, not least the fragrance of passion. Fruits—pomegranate and apricot; flowers—lily and vine blossom; spices—myrrh, cinnamon, aloe; all these waft through the breeze, surrounding the young lovers, heightening their desire. The fragrance-filled garden of delights seems a far cry from the smoke-filled temple of sacrifice.

Chana Bloch and Ariel Bloch, in a new translation of the Song of Songs, describe its springtime setting: "the vines are in blossom, the air is alive with scents and birdsong."[3] Bloch and Bloch believe this poem to be a conversation between two young lovers, unmarried, enamored, innocent. With their colleague Robert Alter, Bloch and Bloch seek to rescue this gem from centuries of interpretation, including both Jewish and Christian efforts to allegorize and chasten its meaning, to tame its erotic sensuality.

The spicy, fruity, flowery perfume of the Song of Songs reveals much about the sensuality of Ancient Israel. Bloch and Bloch remind us that "sex is no sin in the Old Testament," though they acknowledge the Bible's marital strictures.[4] They believe that the Song provides a whiff of reality and of real pleasure: "No wonder," they say, "the pious exegetes of synagogue and church were so quick to marry off the young lovers."[5]

Perhaps the incense of prayer and the scent of passion are not as far apart as we imagine. In both cases the rich luxury of spiciness and the extravagant exuberance of giving are celebrated. The priests offered to God the people's most precious treasures, literally sending them up in smoke. The lovers offer themselves freely to one another, each relishing the sweet smells of the other until their scents are one. The sensuality of smell, in both cases, represents lavish and reciprocal love and devotion, a merging of the sensual and the spiritual. Certainly the Song of Songs has been interpreted as an allegory of divine/ human love, with mixed success, and although its original context seems clearly and concretely sexual, its revelations suggest an erotic dimension to worship and spirituality that has not been lost on mystics throughout the ages.[6]

There are other examples of the link between scent and sensuality in the Hebrew Bible. In the Persian court of Ahasuerus, perfume was used for both the purification and the beautification of the women. Before a girl could go into the king she had a year of cosmetic treatment, with oil of myrrh and perfumes (Esth. 2:12). The finery of the daughters of Zion described by Isaiah includes "perfume boxes and amulets." Judah will be judged for its alien practices and its women humiliated:

> Instead of perfume there will be a stench;
>   and instead of a sash, a rope;
> and instead of well-set hair, baldness;
>   and instead of a rich robe, a binding of sackcloth;
>   instead of beauty, shame. (Isa. 3:24)

The prophet Ezekiel gives us an extended allegory in which the covenantal love of God is likened to that of a husband, Jerusalem to a faithless bride. Again the bride's finery included cleansing and anointing with fragrant oil. "But you trusted your beauty, and played the whore" (Ezek. 16:15), says the prophet on behalf of God. All her rich gifts were lavished on others, including oil and incense, set before other gods "as a pleasing odor" (18–19). In an even more disturbing allegory, the two sisters Oholah and Oholibah represent Samaria and Jerusalem, depicted as wanton harlots, their sexual exploits with foreigners described in lurid detail. Part of their seduction included God's incense and oil, the profaning of holy things (Ezek. 23:41).

There is no feminine form of the word *kohen*, priest, for the priesthood was exclusively male. This fact coupled with allegories such as those in Ezekiel betray the patriarchal nature of ancient Israel and its culture. A feminist approach must view these realities with healthy suspicion. Yet a faithful reader will also be surprised on occasion by the way biblical women used their feminine wiles to expose the hypocrisy of the patriarchs.[7] Sallie McFague notes that many feminists view this patriarchalism—the superiority of a male God and of the godlike male over inferior females—as the root metaphor of Christianity and of biblical faith.[8] While acknowledging the pervasiveness of patriarchalism within Christianity, McFague holds that relationship rather than patriarchy is the root-metaphor of Christian faith.[9] As a Reformed feminist, I would maintain that relationship is the root metaphor of biblical faith, both Hebrew and Christian, and that while patriarchy is a pervasive reality in both Jewish and Christian practice, the seeds of its critique lie within the holy ground of scripture itself.

The imagery of fragrance reveals something of the divine/human relationship. God's Spirit (*ruach*) and God's sense of smell (*re'ach*) are intimately connected. God's nostrils breathe in the smoke of sacrifice, the incense of prayer, the aroma of holy oil. In turn, God's Spirit anoints those God loves: kings like David (Ps. 89:20) and prophets like Isaiah (Isa. 61:1); God's flock (Ps. 23:5) and those who dwell in harmony (Ps. 133). The righteous faithful bear the fragrance of holiness:

> You love righteousness and hate wickedness.
> Therefore God, your God, has anointed you
> with the oil of gladness beyond your companions;
> your robes are all fragrant with myrrh and aloes and cassia.
> (Ps. 45:7, 8)

Divine and human relationships are sometimes mediated with fragrance. Noah's sacrifice was a pleasing odor to God and the occasion of God's promise to preserve life despite human sinfulness (Gen. 8:20–22). On his deathbed, the blind Isaac, meaning to bless his eldest son, Esau, uses all his senses—tasting the food and wine, feeling the hairy hand, hearing his voice, smelling his clothes—yet is deceived by Rebekah's favored son and gives his blessing to Jacob posing as Esau:

> and he smelled the smell of his garments, and blessed him,
>   and said,
> "Ah, the smell of my son
>   is like the smell of a field that the LORD has blessed."
>
> (Gen. 27:27)

Holy smoke wafted above the mercy seat (Lev. 16:12–13); fragrant spices provided a bier for the dead (2 Chr. 16:14); Aaron, his censer full of incense, stood between the living and the dead, stopping a plague (Num. 16:47–48).

The Fragrance of Life and Death

All our relationships, with God, with others, with ourselves, sacred, sensual, are surrounded by the scents and smells, literal and metaphorical, of life and death, of devotion and idolatry, of healing and wounding. As life under Pharaoh was a "bad odor" for the Israelites (Ex. 5:21) and as the odor of idolatry displeased God, so the Christian testament speaks of both stench and perfume, incense and brimstone.

The gospel narratives of Jesus' birth and death are laced with holy and earthy smells. Luke's infancy narrative begins with the priest Zechariah offering incense in the holy of holies, where he receives the angelic message that he will father John the Baptist (Lk. 1:5–23). Though the ox and ass are not mentioned in the gospels, we know that Jesus' birth in a stable must have been awash in animal smells, including those of the shepherds and their sheep and the camels with the caravan. The lavish gifts of the magi at his birth (Mt. 2:11) include myrrh, given later by Nicodemus to embalm him at his death (Jn. 19:39). The gospels tell us that the dying Jesus was offered wine and myrrh as he hung on the cross (Mk. 15:23; cf. Mt. 27:34) and vinegar at the very end (Mt. 27:48; Mk. 15:36).[10] John describes a branch of hyssop, raising a sponge full of sour wine to Jesus' thirsty lips (Jn. 19:29). All four gospels tell of the women who went to the tomb on Easter morning; in two they bring spices to anoint his body (Mk. 16:1; Lk. 24:1).

The most fragrant episode in Jesus' life is his anointing by a woman, told from various vantage points in each of the gospels (Mt.

26:6–13; Mk. 14:3–9; Lk. 7:36–50; Jn. 12:1–8). The variations in the story are as intriguing as the commonalities. Three gospels place the story in Bethany; in Luke it takes place at the home of an unnamed Pharisee. Only John identifies the woman as Mary, sister of Lazarus and Martha; his account sets the story in their home. It is probably Luke's description of the woman as "a sinner" and the verses that follow (Lk. 8:1–3) that have linked this story with Mary Magdalene, a tradition that is not part of the gospel accounts.

In all four stories the woman breaks open a flask of expensive ointment and anoints Jesus' head (Matthew and Mark) or his feet (Luke and John). In each story the male guests protest this action. In Luke, the Pharisees are worried about the woman's sinful condition; in the other three, guests (a disciple in Matthew, Judas in John) are shocked at the extravagance of the act and ask, "Why the waste? For this ointment might have been sold for a large sum, and given to the poor." The answer, "For you always have the poor with you, but you will not always have me," is remembered by all but Luke, who recounts a parable of Jesus about forgiveness which, together with Jesus' forgiveness of the woman, outrages the Pharisees.

Luke places the story early in Jesus' ministry. Elsewhere, the story is a prelude to the passion, for the anointing with ointment is referred to as a preparation for Jesus' burial. It is in Matthew and Mark that Jesus proclaims that the gospel will be preached "in memory of her." In John "the house was filled with the fragrance of the perfume" (Jn. 12:3), a drastic contrast to the stench of Lazarus' own dead body (Jn. 11:39). In light of the all-male priestly tradition, it is striking that all four gospels portray Jesus' anointing by a woman, clearly a sacred, sacramental, subversive act, sanctifying him for the sacrifice to come, while casting both disciples and Pharisees in a critical light. The rich layers of meaning offer us notes also of sin and forgiveness, of worship and devotion, of justice and self-righteousness.

References to the sense of smell in the epistles continue the biblical themes of anointing, sacrifice, and incense. The saints are anointed by the Holy Spirit (2 Cor. 1:21; 1 Jn. 2:20, 27), an anointing that is linked with baptism. James urges elders to anoint the sick (Jas. 5:14), carrying on the apostolic ministry of healing (Mk. 6:13). Gifts offered by the Philippians to Paul in prison are a "fragrant offering," an acceptable sacrifice (Phil. 4:18). The Ephesians are urged to live in love, "as Christ loved us and gave himself up for us, a fragrant offering and sacrifice to God" (Eph. 5:2). Jesus' sacrificial death is the lavish and free gift of God, engendering in us a living sacrifice:

> I appeal to you therefore, brothers and sisters, by the mercies of God, to present your bodies as a living sacrifice, holy and acceptable to God, which is your spiritual worship. Do not be conformed to this world, but be transformed by the renewing of your minds, so that you may discern what is the will of God—what is good and acceptable and perfect.
>
> (Rom. 12:1–2)

This exhortation in Romans and the description of the body of Christ in 1 Corinthians 12, show us that Paul did not always think in dualistic terms. The human body, with all its senses, with all its diversity, unified by the Holy Spirit, is the model for Christ's earthly body, the church. Nose (*osphresis*), eyes, ears, hands, and mouth are all needed for a sensing of the Spirit that is whole and complete. Later, Paul describes the saints as the aroma (*euodia*) of Christ, bearing the fragrance of life in a world that reeks of death (2 Cor. 2:15–16).

The smells of life and death permeate the book of Revelation as well. The heavenly host bear golden bowls of incense, representing the prayers of the saints, but seven angels also bear golden bowls containing the wrath of God, which, when poured out, plagues the earth (Rev. 16). Even as the sweet incense of prayer fills the air (5:8; 8:3; 15:8; 18:13), the stench of fire and brimstone rise from the bottomless pit (9:2), the horses' mouths (9:17), the destruction of Babylon (18:9, 18), and the lake of fire (19:20; 20:10; 21:8).

Anointed Anointing

Though biblical worship is aromatic and though Christian worship throughout the ages has included incense and fragrant oil, our modern sensibilities, particularly our Protestant sensibilities, have either ignored or resisted the olfactory. Geoffrey Wainwright offers a cultural explanation for the universality of bread, wine, and water and the abandonment of oil and anointing in certain places:

> Oil, and particularly olive oil, is less universal in its use and associations with healing, health, beauty, blessing, and appointment to office and honour. Could it be that the 'protestant' abandonment of its use in initiation, ordination and the sacrament of the sick was due at least in part to a Northern failure to appreciate the Mediterranean commodity?[11]

Our ecumenical age has freed us to consider our common roots in the pre-Reformation tradition and to reconsider the richness of symbolic elements viewed as suspect by our Protestant forbears. Wainwright notes not only "scriptural resonance" for the practice of anointing in the rites of the church but also reminds us that, "It is as close to Christianity as the title given to Jesus, the Spirit-anointed Christ."[12] A brief consideration of "initiation, ordination, and the sacrament of the sick" in the early church may help us recover the ancient and sensual practice of anointing with fragrant oil.

Just as oil and spices were an oblation, an offering of the people to their God in the worship of the temple, oblations were made in early Christian worship. A key source for many of the church's liturgical practices is the *Apostolic Tradition* of Hippolytus, a document said to contain "the model of all liturgies known to us."[13] Dating to the early third century, this document contains perhaps the earliest post-biblical evidence for the uses of oil in Christian worship. In the eucharistic service, gifts of bread, wine, oil, cheese, olives, milk, and honey are offered by the people and *"eucharistized,"* blessed with thanksgiving. While Protestants seem to have no problem including an offering of money in our services of worship, often placing the plates directly on the communion table, many view the offering of the communion elements as "sacrificial," and thus unacceptable. The giving of earthy elements, of worldly goods, to God in worship seems a fitting way to practice a biblical and historical faith.

Hippolytus' prayer of thanksgiving for the oil connects it with biblical rites of anointing: "O God who sanctifies this oil, as Thou dost grant unto all who are anointed and receive of it the hallowing wherewith Thou didst anoint kings and priests and prophets, so grant that it may give strength to all that taste of it and health to all that use it."[14] Anointing with oil was an important part of early Christian initiation; Hippolytus describes both pre- and post-baptismal anointing.[15] Two deacons assist the priest, the one on his left administering the "oil of exorcism" after the renunciation of evil and before the initiate enters the water. A deacon accompanies the new believer into the water where he or she receives threefold baptism as the articles of the creed are recited. When the newly baptized emerges from the water, the oil of thanksgiving is administered.[16]

Cyril of Jerusalem refers to Christian initiation in fragrant terms:

> Already the savour of bliss is upon you, who have come to be enlightened [those to be baptized at the end of Lent]; you

have begun to pluck spiritual flowers with which to weave heavenly crowns. Already are you redolent of the fragrance of the Holy Spirit. You have reached the royal vestibule…Lo, now the trees are in blossom; and grant the fruit be duly gathered.[17]

Though both young children and those of age were baptized in the early church, confirmation or chrismation eventually became a separate rite. Whereas baptism was sealed with the holy unction of the Spirit, as infant baptism became the norm, anointing with oil and balm was more closely linked with confirmation and ordination. Much controversy has followed from the separation of the two rites, baptism being linked with forgiveness of sins, confirmation with the receiving of the gifts of the Spirit.[18]

Anointing of the sick is also given early evidence. Not only the blessing of the oil in the *Apostolic Tradition*, but the fourth-century *Sacramentary* of Serapion contains a prayer for the oil of anointing,

for a driving out of all fever and ague and every infirmity, for good grace and remission of sins, for a medicine of life and salvation, for health and soundness of soul, body, spirit, for perfect strengthening.[19]

The sacrament of extreme unction, by which only those *in extremis* were anointed, came into practice in the twelfth century. Not surprisingly, the Reformers objected to the separation of such unction from its biblical purpose of healing: "James wishes all sick persons to be anointed; these fellows smear with their grease not the sick but half dead corpses when they are already drawing their last breath," quips Calvin.[20] It seems a hopeful sign that both Catholic and Protestant practices once again see a connection between anointing and healing, between spiritual and bodily health and wholeness, a connection that also views death as a sacramental moment.[21]

Textual Scents and Senses

My father, the fragrance merchant, reminds me that to really take in and identify a scent takes a certain focused and concentrated process. One breathes deeply through the nose, clearing it of any aromatic residue. A small felt wand is dipped into the bottle and waved in a circular motion beneath the nostrils. Breathing in slowly and intently, the subject is to identify as many "notes" as possible in the sample—the first blush, the middle notes, and the bottom, or lasting aroma. Any given sample has several notes, identifiable by professionals, elusive to most of us. Perfumers and oenologists do have a specialized vocabulary for these variants, but even their words refer to other senses: oaky, grassy, fruity, sharp, harsh, flat.

It seems to me that the challenge of interpreting a multivalent scent is something like the venture of interpreting a polyvalent text, though the form and shape of a fragrance are much harder to define than the genre of a text. We have noted the manifold fragrances wafting through the Song of Songs; even more profuse are the layers of interpretation heaped upon this love poem. Ann Matter rightly claims that the Christian commentaries on this text, particularly those of the medieval period, constitute a sub-genre of their own, the interpretive texts themselves forming a special place in literary history.[22]

Ann Matter's views on the original sense of this poem tend to resonate with those of Chana Bloch and Ariel Bloch and of Robert Alter.[23] "The curiously blatant eroticism of the Song of Songs," she contends, "is one of the most obvious features of the text, a feature that has aroused in some twentieth-century scholars a basic mistrust of the medieval tradition of allegorical interpretation."[24] Matter is interested in genre, and she concurs with those who view genre as shaped by historical contexts. She begins her study of the Song of Songs and its interpretation with Origen and deftly shows how the poem's exegesis has been rooted in the settings of its commentators.

Origen was, of course, known for a Neoplatonism that viewed everything in threes—God, human nature, exegesis. His three senses of scripture—historical, spiritual, and mystical—corresponded to body, soul, and spirit. As the rabbis viewed the Song as an allegory of God and Israel, Christian exegetes, beginning with Origen, read it as an allegory of Christ and the Church. Matter shows how Origen's Latin *Homilies* and *Commentary* on the Song influenced Jerome, Ambrose, and later Latin commentaries. Matter cites Origen's commentary on verse 1:3 ("your name is oil poured out," in the Vulgate) as a model:

> One might well see in the same words a prophecy pronounced
> by the Bride about Christ, that it would come to pass at the
> advent of our Lord and Savior that his name would thus be

spread about through the orb of the earth, and through the entire world, that there would be "an odor of sweetness in every place," as the Apostle says: "We are the good odor of Christ in every place; to the one indeed the odor of death unto death, but to others the odor of life unto life."[25]

The allegorizing of the medieval commentators added layers of meaning to the poem and to Origen's foundation, though they viewed themselves as drawing meaning from an inspired text: "The Song of Songs was consistently interpreted by medieval exegetes along the lines of a series of assumed meanings placed in the text by the Holy Spirit, meanings which could only be made clear through the process of allegorical interpretation."[26] Matter shows how these allegorists, Honorius, Bede, Gregory the Great, and the popular Haimo of Auxerre added their words to the gloss. All built upon the hermeneutics of Augustine and Cassian, who expanded Origen's three to a fourfold sense of scripture, viewing the Holy Spirit as the author, Solomon as the human scribe of the marriage song of Christ and Ecclesia, an *ecclesia* that looked a lot like the idealized medieval church, pure and spotless Bride of Christ.[27]

Like Bloch and Bloch, Matter believes the Song fared better when mystics like Bernard of Clairvaux began to read it as a spiritual song of the love between God and the individual soul, the search for mystical union. Though Bernard follows earlier exegetes, especially Origen, Matter suggests that "his understanding of the biblical text is worked out in a primarily spiritual mode."[28] Bernard wrote some eighty homilies, or sermons, on the Song, never moving beyond verse 3:1. These sermons have an orality to them that conveys the personal engagement of Bernard with the text and with his audience, his fellow monks at Clairvaux. Though the allegory of mystical marriage between Christ, the Word-made-flesh, and the believer is present throughout, and though he moves through the Song of Songs verse by verse, Bernard's sermons depart from the exegetical genre of the commentaries, becoming a guide for Cistercian spirituality.[29]

The exegetes focused on the allegory of Christ and the Church; the Latin liturgical tradition viewed Mary as the Song's bride.[30] The spiritual marriage of Word and soul expounded by Bernard became the basis of the *Brautmystik*. This nuptial mysticism viewed Christ as lover, soul as Bride, their union as erotic, sensual. Both male and female mystics viewed themselves as Christ's female lover, though at times the suffering Christ took on a female attraction.[31] It is common among women mystics to speak of this mystical marriage; Catherine of Siena's marriage to Christ was sealed with the ring of his circumcised foreskin, invisible to all but her.

The basis of an erotic spirituality can be found in these texts that read the Song of Songs in terms of nuptial mysticism. Feminist and womanist theologians from Audre Lorde to Carter Heyward to Rita Nakashima Brock have sought to reclaim the erotic for contemporary faith. Heyward calls the erotic, "our most fully embodied experience of the love of God."[32] Brock calls it the "power of our primal interrelatedness."[33] Not surprisingly, there is some controversy among feminist scholars about the value of medieval eroticism, for its nuptial imagery is seen to be based on hierarchical relations between the sexes and patriarchal gender stereotypes.[34]

This brings us back to the matter of interpretation and the challenge of making sense of ancient texts in modern times. Our fragrant metaphor reminds us that though unraveling the notes, moving through the layers of gloss, is difficult, there are a lasting residue, a scent that remains with these classic texts, not always easily recognizable or speakable but conveying meaning into future times and contexts. Perhaps more difficult to discern are the idiosyncratic scents that we bring as modern-day readers to these musty tomes and times; it is to this challenge that we turn.

Pungent Protest

Growing up Protestant always seemed a fairly neutral thing to me. As I absorbed the culture of my family's faith, certain truths seemed timeless, transparent. Catholic women wore pants to church; we didn't. My best friend fasted and went to confession before Mass; I talked to God one on one. She went to catechism, I memorized Bible verses in Sunday school. School lunches on Fridays were usually fishsticks or macaroni and cheese, in deference to a quirky Catholic custom. Once I got a whiff of church history, Calvin and Luther and Zwingli and Knox became great heroes to me, cleansing the church of relics and superstition, of statues and smoke. Even as a graduate student, I was grateful for the inroads of these heroes who had begun a process that enabled me to become a minister, while my Catholic sisters were forbidden, allowed only as far as the convent.

Gradually my studies introduced me to the far-reaching work of Catholic women in theology and biblical studies and liturgy and spirituality. It occurred to me that my Catholic sisters still held the power of dissent and protest and loyal opposition, while my newly ordained power was part of the system, a system hardly devoid of patriarchy. It was only when I prepared to teach a seminary course on Women in the Age of Reformation, in a Protestant seminary, that I got a real sniff of my clan's odor. As I looked for texts and stories of sixteenth- century women, I began to sense that the Reformers bore the scent of life to some, the stench of death to others.

Roland Bainton's volumes on *Women in the Reformation* introduced me to German women like Katherine Zell and Käthe von Bora and to French women like Marguerite of Navarre and her daughter, Jeanne d'Albert.[35] I eagerly learned their stories and searched for their texts, often difficult to track down. Katherine Zell impressed me as a gutsy woman, wife of a Strasbourg Reformer. When forced to defend her speaking and writing she said, "I do not pretend to be John the Baptist rebuking the Pharisees, I do not claim to be Nathan upbraiding David, I aspire only to be Balaam's ass, castigating his master."[36] The story of Luther and his compatriots "liberating" nuns from the convent and taking them for wives seemed most romantic to me, especially the part where the women were secreted away in herring barrels.[37] Calvin's correspondence with famous and courtly women, queens and duchesses who joined and supported his movement, only raised him in my esteem.[38]

Yet I began to wonder if all these women viewed their liberation as liberating. Was Katherina von Bora really better off as Luther's wife than she was as a Cistercian nun? Was the move "from cloister to kitchen" really a step forward?[39] The texts of two Roman Catholic nuns, one from Nuremberg, the other from Geneva, helped clear the air, introducing a perspective previously foreign to my Protestant senses.

Barbara Pirckheimer was born in 1467, the eldest child in a well-to-do Bavarian family. Joining the *Klarakloster* in Nuremberg in 1483, she took the name Caritas. In 1503 she was made abbess, a position she held when the city was declared Protestant in 1525. The city council soon began closing monasteries and convents, and on June 7, Caritas and the nuns received articles of compliance, demanding that all sisters be freed of their vows, allowed to return to their families and to dress in secular clothing. The nuns were ordered to install windows so visiting relatives could see and be seen and to present an inventory of their possessions.[40] Caritas' text is a moving account of the very real struggle of these Catholic sisters with their Protestant relatives. The abbess appears faithful and wise and the Reformers and their tactics ruthless and even sacrilegious. Though a number of nuns were forced to leave against their will, only one left voluntarily. Most conversation and correspondence between the abbess and the reformers was fairly hostile and futile, but Caritas speaks well of a meeting with Phillip Melanchthon, who put an end to the violence and granted the sisters some measure of peace.

Caritas describes a confrontation on the feast of Corpus Christi, the convent being forced to "free" three daughters of Lutheran converts: "So around eleven o'clock the wild wolves and the she-wolves came among my beloved little sheep, entered the church, pushed all the people outside, and bolted the church shut." Caritas was determined to allow the mothers to speak freely to their daughters, in the privacy of the convent chapel. "There among the she-wolves stood my poor little orphans struggling with all their might...I had freed their children, and they could see how willingly they came out." The mothers begged Caritas to dissolve their vows, which she would not, could not do. The daughters spoke, "We don't want to be freed of our vows, rather we want to keep our vows to God with His help." Eventually the young nuns were removed forcibly, with some violence, with much weeping and wailing, and in the full view of many townspeople. So much for Luther's "liberation" of the convents.

Things were much the same in Geneva, it would seem. The Swiss city was a haven for refugees, Reformed Christians escaping religious persecution in France and Britain, in particular. Yet the Protestant refugees seemed to have little sympathy for Catholics dwelling in their fair city. Like Caritas, Jeanne de Jussie was a sister of Saint Clare who wrote an account of her convent's struggles with the Protestants in Geneva from 1526 to 1535.[41] Her text tells us much about life within the convent and about key figures in the religious struggles of the time. She paints a picture of devout sisters seeking to live their religious life amid constant interruptions and harassing distractions from the "Syndics" and their sympathizers. The nuns were very literally defending their faith against an onslaught which they viewed as heretical. As in Nuremberg, Protestant relatives were among those eager to remove the nuns from their convent.

According to Sister Jeanne, "they haven't ceased even a single day from sending someone from their sect to trouble and spy on the poor nuns, and often they would say scurrilous and detestable words."[42] Like the Nurembergers, the Genevan Reformers believed that nuns were held in the convent against their will and would readily leave if allowed to hear "the truth of the Gospel." "Sirs, save your grace," the nuns replied, "for we have all come inspired by the grace of the Holy Spirit and not by constraint...We are not all hypocrites, as you say, but pure virgins." It seems the nuns had a real fear of forced marriage, preferring their chaste way of life. In the course of her account, Jeanne de Jussie introduces her readers to Calvin's predecessor, Guillaume Farel, to his colleagues Viret and Fromment, and to the female Reformer, Marie Dentière, all extremely unsympathetic characters in the eyes of Jeanne and her sisters. In the end, the sisters relocated to Annecy, France, where Sister Jeanne became abbess. The stench was ultimately too much for them.

Contemporary Conversations

Reflection on the sense of smell, on the ways we detect the Spirit's scent and our own, the ways the imagery of fragrant aroma and pungent odor helps us in our spiritual and theological musings, circles back on the beginning of this venture, to *ruach* and the power to hear and speak God's Word. I find the sense of smell an apt metaphor for a hermeneutic approach to scripture and tradition and to the way these texts are perceived in faithful, embodied life.

As the notes of any fragrance are available to the nose, so the sacred text of the Bible is a given but elusive gift. It comes out of life and experience into life and experience, yet the smell of its bloom is new and constant whenever, wherever it is opened and taken in. As faithful interpreters, we have the ability to sharpen our skills as do the scent professionals. Yet the text will bear meaning even to those without the training of exegete, hermeneut, linguist. The Bible is an anthology of genres, an interpretation of interpretations, for the words on the page represent the lived lives of a whole company of embodied, Spirit-filled faithful.

Though scripture is polyvalent, thick and deep with truth, bearing to generations what Ricoeur calls a "surplus of meaning," not all meanings gleaned are faithful.[43] Our challenge is to read both scripture and tradition faithfully into our experience. Some have suggested that the right methodology will ensure right reading, but in the science of smell, complicated techniques are of little help when the scent is actually wafting through the nostrils. If God's Spirit is present with us, if God's Spirit has been present with the people of God in all times and places, then the Spirit who abides within us in front of the text is also behind it.[44]

Faithfulness involves both trust and suspicion. We bring our creedal stance, our clan's scent, to all our sense-making. It is an act of faith to assume that God's Spirit inhabits human authors and readers. But we must bring our doubts and questions with us, not only to the biblical authors or to those who have interpreted it through the ages, but to ourselves as well. False consciousness is something like believing ourselves to be odorless. It may well be that only "others" can help us to identify our own scent, to unmask our notion that we are "fragrance free." It is probably impossible to clear the nostrils altogether, to deodorize ourselves. And so we acknowledge the peculiar scents we bring to the process, paying attention to how they shape our reading and understanding and response.

Our consideration of those "fragrant" passages of scripture and of their interpretation in Christian history suggest two additional themes for an embodied spirituality in current reflection: healing and prayer.

The Holy Spirit is a healing Spirit, for health and holiness, wholeness and healing, are interconnected, not just linguistically. Biblical faith revolves around the promotion of right relationship and well-being, of salvation, *salus,* of God's *shalom.* Isaiah offers this vision of shalom, a vision echoed in the ministry of Jesus:

> Then the eyes of the blind shall be opened,
> and the ears of the deaf unstopped;
> then the lame shall leap like a deer,
> and the tongue of the speechless sing for joy. (Isa. 35:5–6)

Yet such wholeness, such restoration of the senses, bodily and spiritual, is not fully realized.

We live in an age obsessed with healing, perhaps because it seems so elusive. A quick survey of the alternative healing section of the bookstore reminded me that there are therapies for every kind of ill and therapies which make use of each of our senses in healing—music therapy, massage therapy, herbal therapy, art therapy, aromatherapy.

Aromatherapy attaches healing power to some three hundred essential oils, all extracted from plants and believed capable of alleviating everything from stress to addiction, from depression to amnesia. In an age when even the medical profession is exploring alternatives and when spiritual/somatic connections are being explored in new ways, the healing power of scent may be more than quackery or New Age craftiness. In fact, many of the essences used in aromatherapy are those same scents valued in scripture—frankincense, spikenard, sandalwood, cassia, myrtle, hyssop.

Sacrifice and offering, incense and anointing, are the Spirit's healing fragrance, the aroma of life when practiced in faithfulness. In ministering to God, in serving God, the priests ministered to the people of God; in offering her richest gift, the woman anointed Jesus for his death on our behalf. Healing of body, of mind, of spirit also entails healing of relationships, bringing forgiveness and reconciliation and ultimately preparing us for death and new life. Could it be that the Spirit's gifts of healing are manifest in Lourdes and in Los Angeles, in the hands of the Pentecostal preacher and the Sisters of Charity? She blows where she wills.

So we pray. Our prayers are like incense, filling the temple, rising toward heaven. Our prayers are an anointing, a taking in of God's presence, God's holiness. Yet all too often our prayer life and our theological reflection are at odds. We offer intercessions, but we confess God to be impassible, above it all. We ask for guidance, but we hold that the future is in God's hands. We struggle to break free from oppressive and idolatrous worship, yet our public prayers are thick with *gloria patris* and *pater noster*s.

Two books by two women, theologians writing about prayer, have helped me in my own wrestlings. Both Marjorie Suchocki and Roberta Bondi move out of their usual genres to reflect theologically on the life of prayer.[45] Both work to integrate language and imagery for God with the reality of relationship in prayer. We often view God as genie or king, suggests Suchocki, hoarding or bestowing power as the case may be. "But if this is an interdependent world, then just as surely as we receive from God, God receives from us…Prayer in such a world is an openness to God's own creative energy, and to the good that God intends for us. It is also an offering back to God, giving God the gift of ourselves."[46]

Suchocki wrestles also with the Lord's Prayer and its naming of God as our "father." With other feminists, she sees the exclusive use of "father" for God as idolatrous, deifying masculinity. Yet she sees in the name "our" father an equalization, an overturning of privilege and rank, and not just those based on gender: "The 'ourness' of the relation to father overturns the patriarchal privilege of 'your' father against 'mine,'" writes Suchocki, "Jesus replaced social privilege with the humble privilege of the Spirit."[47]

Roberta Bondi also struggles with the fatherhood, and the motherhood, of God. Her struggle is intimately connected with her own familial relations, as all spiritual and theological struggles must be. She is bold to share these intimate connections with her readers: "It is not enough for me to know that I am made, a generic human being, in the image of God who is my Father. I am a woman, and I must know that the image of God in which I am made is also the image of God who is my mother."[48] This struggle was intensified by her parents' unequal relationship, by her earthly father's put-downs, and by the church:

> This being so, how could I have ever known to conceive of God as mother? In all my memories of my Presbyterian Sunday school and of the revivals at my grandparents' Pond Fork Baptist Church it was the perfect God the Father I heard about. To speak of God as mother would, by definition, have imported all this female imperfection into God. I was afraid of God, and with good reason.[49]

The power of prayer is the power to heal both memories and relationships; a life of prayer is a life in the Spirit, the Spirit of the God who is parent and friend, creator and breath of life. All our prayers, formal and poetic, impromptu and anguished, are a pleasing odor to God, for they sanctify a living relationship, one which returns to us the aroma of life.

As a pastor I struggle with prayer, with the different ways people ask and expect me to pray, with the dissonance, at times, between my theological self, my liturgical self, and my everyday self. Whenever I prayed in the gothic high kirk of St. Giles, I composed my prayers well ahead of time and wrote them down, even when offered at noontime to the empty vaults, for somehow I felt my words must match the history and the mystery of that place. When I step into the congregation of a small country church in Indiana each Sunday and ask for joys and concerns, I make up the prayers as I go along, fitting my words to the folks I serve, who most often want to pray for the safety and health of friends and family and sometimes even for the world God loves. Their prayers, like the incense in the temple, are the very fragrance of life. Thanks be to God who is both immanent and transcendent, both here and there, whose Spirit is present in cathedral and chapel, who translates our words into the language of that same Spirit.

Conclusion

Making Sense

Theology is sense-making; it is making sense of texts and traditions within the contexts of lived life—the lived life of faith. Texts, traditions, and lives are concrete—earthen vessels bearing truth and wisdom. Ancient texts, historical texts can be bridges or windows into the lives and contexts of others in times and places distant from our own. We know now that times and texts and lives and traditions are open to interpretation but that faithful reading will struggle to learn about the worlds behind and within the text, even as such reading is rooted in the present.

This sense-making venture has itself produced new insights into the process of interpretation. Sensory perception alone offers little by way of certitude, for it involves always an embodied perspective that is unique and idiosyncratic. Sense has become for us both a figurative and a literal way of knowing, but more a hermeneutic than an epistemology. Yet there is a kind of common sense, a sensing that, when done with others in community, in conversation with other times and *loci,* begins to bring perception, perspective into focus. By using all our senses, by listening to others whose senses are keener, by remembering that sensing involves at least two parties, we have a chance of transcending our idiosyncrasies.

This sense-making reflection is systemic, not systematic, theology. More organic than detached, more relational than disinterested, more circular than disconnected, systemic thought finds it impossible to concentrate on one thing at a time. The human body is itself a prime model for a systemic approach, for it is a system of systems, as is creation itself. No matter the starting point—skeletal, nervous, digestive, adrenal, circulatory, respiratory—one encounters always connections with other possible starting points. Systemic theology is heuristic in that it is a voyage of discovery, hoping always to gain new insight even while traveling familiar ground.

Systemic thought circles back upon itself, but within an open system. For a systemic theologian, the circumference of mystery is ever-expanding, defying reduction, deduction. As we learn, new questions are raised. We find that the rabbis are right—questions are answers, answers questions. Rather than concentration, which focuses on a still point at the center, systemic thought is eccentric; it moves outward, flirting with mystery, a spiral. Yet it is centered in particularity—embodied, indwelt, creaturely existence.[1]

As adjectives modify nouns, so real persons, places, and things are modified by the names we give them, the names we choose for ourselves, and perhaps by the epithets others assign to us. Adjectives modify, they shape our thinking, they identify our mode of reflection as theologians. I have said that my approach is more hermeneutic than epistemological, more systemic than systematic, and so I am compelled to name and acknowledge my perspective. The two adjectives I have most often used to modify my reflection, to describe my location, are "Reformed" and "feminist."[2] These adjectives represent for me the hermeneutic circle: suspicion and trust, trust and suspicion.

I am Reformed because my faith was shaped in the culture of Presbyterianism. Baptized as an infant, my parents kept their promise to raise me in the "nurture and admonition" of the Lord. I learned to love the Bible, to trust it, to find it trustworthy "in matters of faith and practice," though not, in the end, infallible or inerrant. The church has been a home to me, a familiar place, a continuity. Within Reformed Protestantism, I also found the seeds of dissent and the freedom to disagree, to think for myself, for when I was ordained an elder I learned that my opinion matters, that "God alone is Lord of the conscience." Reformed for me has meant a rooting in the holy ground of scripture and a lively engagement with the traditions that have sprung from that ground.[3]

As I grew up in this Presbyterian church, in my branch of the "Reformed tradition," I also learned about patriarchy. God's grace was for all, as long as I thought of myself as part of "all men." God is a kind and gracious father, as long as I thought of myself as a "son" of God. As for other women in the church, this dawned on me gradually and then with a great force. When I finally sought ordination as a minister, I grieved the fact that it took me so long to hear the Spirit's voice, having never seen or heard a woman minister in any of the churches where my faith was nurtured. And so a budding feminism offered me a healthy suspicion of church and tradition and even of the Bible.

For me, bringing my feminist, Reformed Christian faith to my theological reflection means that I must be at once critical and constructive, faithful and skeptical. It means that I will suspect patriarchy in the biblical context and in my own, but it means that I will look beyond that for the deeper truth of right relations. In this reflection on Spirit, on Holy Spirit, on divine and human spirits, my Reformed feminist perspective has engaged me in a struggle with dualisms, trusting in parallelism and paradox but suspicious of dual standards that sanctify privilege, whether of gender or class or race or religion, including my own. I realize all too well that the usable past that has helped with my sense-making is very much *my* usable past.

A Theology of Spirit

Just what have we learned about the Holy Spirit by way of this sense-making venture? We have listened to her voice; we have tilled the soil of scripture; we have partaken of her feast, felt the warmth of her fire, sniffed her presence. By searching for sensual imagery for Spirit, we have been able, I hope, to move beyond the numinous, ghostly, and impersonal Spirit familiar to more conventional theology. Yet the Spirit we have sensed bears some resemblance to traditional pictures.

We began with new birth, with the breath of life, the sound of crying and speech. The Spirit is a mighty wind and a still, small voice. God's Spirit gives both prophetic utterance and faith-filled hearing; she translates divine speech into language we can understand. The Holy Spirit bears witness with our spirits, enabling our speaking, our testimony, our proclamation and praise. God's inspiring, encouraging Spirit empowers prophetic action—both words and deeds. In this sense, the Spirit's wind is a movement of integration, of wholeheartedness, of the union of *nephesh* and *levav,* heart and soul, spirit and body. She breaks into oppressive history and tradition in radical and surprising manifestations, sometimes in the teachings of the orthodox, often at the margins rather than the mainstream, even at times in heresy and herstory.

Our observations of the Spirit in nature and in the green imagery of scripture and tradition focus us on the creating, recreating energy of God's Spirit. The cycles of nature are cycles of birth, death, and resurrection, so the Spirit's life in us gives growth and newness and hope in the face of death and decay. As earthworms transform nature's refuse into rich soil, so God's Spirit changes, remakes, redeems. The Spirit of creation is constantly at work restoring right relations, giving exiles roots, making the barren fruitful, nurturing creativity and imagination. This green, growing Spirit is creator, recreator, resurrection power.

"The world is charged with the grandeur of God," wrote Hopkins[4]; as creativity enlivens nature, so all of creation longs for God's Spirit as for home or food or friendship. Reflection on the sense of taste, on the imagery of hunger and thirst, helps us sense the deep connections between bodily desire and spiritual longing. Right relation with God's Spirit enables enjoyment of creaturely comforts, pleasure and satiety, gratitude and temperance. Too much of a good thing, whether wine or sex, chocolate or music, can harm us spiritually, for such excess can quench our hunger for God. Deprivation can hurt us both physically and spiritually, damaging all our relationships. God's Spirit offers us deep satisfaction, sanctifies our deepest desires, provides for all our needs, frees us to venture out in love.

The sense of touch conjures up Spirit-images of heat and fire, consuming as well as comforting. God's presence is a blazing presence, for God's Spirit rests with us and remains with us as fiery pillar or burning bush. The Spirit's dwelling among us, with us, within us, touches us with holiness, burning away our failures and betrayals. God's fiery anger kindles in us passion and compassion, for heartfelt spirituality is a jealous longing for justice and reconciliation. Our covenant partnership with the Holy Spirit is mediated by the sparks of divinity that burn between us and God; we are changed by God's glowing, and we have a part in the manifestation of God's glory.

The breath of life, the *ruach* of God, evokes also the fragrance of life that is the Spirit's distinctive odor. The Spirit is ubiquitous but remains truly personal. God's lavish love for us is reflected in the service and worship and prayer offered by the faithful in all times and places.

The divine/human relationship is surrounded with spicy scents, the smells of love and longing, of confession and forgiveness, of health and wholeness. Like perfume, God's Spirit is mysteriously present, discerning, interceding, counseling, healing. This same Spirit aids our perception, sharpens our self-awareness, reminds us of others who need gifts of love and offerings of service.

The Holy Spirit is Mighty Wind, Breath of Life, Creative Energy, Sanctifier, Holy Fire, Comforter, Heart's Desire, Healing Presence. These are tangible, earthy, biblical, traditional names for God the Spirit. We have also sensed the Spirit to be Witness-Bearer, Prophetic Speech, Greening Gardener, Midwife of New Birth, Satisfying Food, Passionate Lover, Uppity Woman, Saving Grace, Spice of Life. She is powerful, present, loving, imaginative, universal, wise. She is freedom itself, yet chooses an embodied life, an earthly abode, making creation her home.

Certainly this utterly free Spirit is not bound by the walls of the institutions we call the church, visible or invisible. She appeared long before Pentecost and was hardly absent in the history of Israel, or of any other history for that matter. Nor did her activity cease when the canon of Scripture was settled (thank God!), for inspiration must work in the process of interpretation as well, even in the writings and prayers, the confessions and sermons of fallible, faithful witnesses to this day. God the Spirit, ubiquitous as she can be, is the most "portable" member of the Trinity in the sense that she is the very presence, the real presence of God, God-with-us, living Word, Lord, and Giver of Life.[5]

The Spirit of Theology

So now we move from pneumatology to Trinitarian thought, from a theology of Spirit to other *loci,* yet by way of Spirit nonetheless. I will resist the urge to go back and compose a mini-systematic in creedal form, though this is a kind of a credo. Rather I will return once more to the five senses, this time to discover what a relational system that starts with Spirit might reveal.

Reflection on the sense of sound has much to teach about proclamation, revelation, and anthropology. *Ruach* as breath, wind, and spirit breathes and blows through human being and sacred script, making human speech at times holy and prophetic. Our consideration of Hebrew anthropology seeks to reassert the unity, the integrity of the whole human being created in the divine image. We are to love God, ourselves, our neighbors wholeheartedly, with body, mind, spirit. Creation in God's image is not limited to male human beings but manifest also in spirited women, who have dared to bear witness with their bodies and their voices to the Spirit's life. We are, all of us, carnate, loved, inspired.

Scripture is God-breathed; it is inspired in that God's Spirit is behind it and within it and before it, for God's Spirit permeates the lives of the faithful, those that spoke, wrote, redacted, translated, compiled, copied, interpreted the sacred text. Revelation comes to us not in a vacuum but through the medium of living, breathing creaturely existence. It rings true for us because there is an earthly connection between our life of faith and those who live in the pages of the Bible. Wholehearted, God-breathed life in the Spirit enables us to bear witness to the truth we find there, empowers prophetic preaching and hearing, and encourages us to argue, to speak, and to listen, even, especially to the silences of history.

Focus on greenness, on the Spirit-images of growth and nature, is also reflection on creation, providence, and evil. Creation is a mixture of beauty and violence, of order and chaos. Both the primordial garden and the eschatological garden possess a sense of shalom and well-being that is incomplete in the present. The cycles of nature are miraculous, but they often betray us. Yet faithful participation calls us as creatures to work with God in the creation of shalom, to see God's providence as a cooperative effort between a God who made and loves creation and beloved creatures whose faithful response is the promotion of well-being. Faith helps us to see that resurrection is an essential part of the created order.

Spiritual sight is about growth in grace; it is reflection on the whole web of life with the eyes of faith. Vision teaches us about the divine/human relationship, about providence and redemption, and it teaches us about the relationships between God's Word and God's creation. Both creation and the Bible bear truth, the Word giving focus to the world, the ground of scripture bearing fruit and seed for faithful living. The sense of sight is also about perspective, about the limits of our horizons, and about the need for community in the task of seeing and sense-making.

Reflection on the sense of taste is about sin and the sacraments. It is about sin because it is about all kinds of desire—for God and for that which is not God. Our fleshly desires are not essentially sinful, only when those desires supplant, or quench, our desire for God does sin enter in. The Spirit-filled life is a life where creaturely pleasures are enjoyed as gifts from God, where God is the object of our deepest desire and longing. The brokenness of sin—addiction, abuse, violence—is manifest when we try to satisfy our longing for God with that which is not God, when we worship the creation rather than the Creator.

The sense of taste is also a taste for the sacraments, for the rites that offer us a foretaste of things to come. Water, wine, and bread represent the basic necessities of life. The waters of baptism cleanse and refresh; they allow us to participate in death to sin and a rising to new life; they offer us a welcome, a belonging, an initiation into the Spirit-filled life. Communion is food for life; it is both bitter and sweet, offering as it does both crucifixion and resurrection, body broken and blood poured out, bread of heaven, cup of salvation. In these two sacraments we literally sense the Spirit, taking her in, entering her presence, offering thanks. Sin and sacrament, longing and satisfaction point us toward God's future, a future of hope and fulfillment.

God's fiery Spirit evokes in us both warm comfort and stifling heat, for the sense of touch is about both judgment and acceptance. It is impossible to escape the reality of God's commanding holiness, the indignant reaction of a loving, relational God to betrayal, idolatry, and injustice. Anger is a very real attribute of God and one that shows God as present and engaged with humanity. Without judgment, God's grace is divorced from the ethical. Unless God's love reacts against violence and hate, it is a love devoid of holiness, of reparation. We face the future with hope but facing the burning heat of the Spirit's refining. Righteous anger is a divine gift, one that can easily burn out of control, but tepid faith and lukewarm love lack the fervor and the fiery passion of heartfelt holiness.

Holy fire is not always discomforting, it can also be hospitable, welcoming. The church is spoken of as holy, and often this has meant judgmental and exclusive, but holiness also reflects wholeness, and the church is whole only in its diversity. The sense of touch leads to reflection on the wildly diverse ways that the Spirit's holy fire burns in the world. The Spirit makes us one precisely because she makes a home within our radical particularity. She is at home with Pentecostals and Presbyterians; she abides in Russian patriarchs and Korean women. The church's holiness is no guarantee of its infallibility; history has demonstrated that. Nor is the church holy because she possesses the Spirit; our reflection on Hebrew history has debunked that claim. If the church is holy, it is because God's Spirit chooses to make a home among us and to bind us together whatever our peculiarities.

The connections between wholeness and holiness are also evoked as we consider the sense of smell, for the Bible is full of holy smells that consecrate and heal. Spiritual fragrance teaches us about prayer, about priestly prayer and sacrifice, about the incense of worship and devotion, and about the healing power of prayer. Just as incense and fragrant oil consecrate tabernacle and temple, as believers we are anointed with the fragrance of new life, of living into wholeness. As God has lavished upon us all manner of blessings, so we offer God all we are and have, out of gratitude rather than guilt, as free gift, as rich praise. Since the Spirit makes her home with us, she also hears and translates those prayers that arise from the very real pain of human existence, the cries of anguish and despair that also are prayers of lamentation and mourning.

So we have circled around the familiar places of theological reflection with Spirit as our point of entry. Thoughts on revelation and proclamation have been voiced, along with those on human nature. Creation, providence, and evil have been observed along with insights into a hermeneutic approach. We have sampled the sacraments and pondered sin and forgiveness. We have touched on the church and the holy judgment to come. All along we have breathed in the life of the Spirit, noting that pneumatology and spirituality, the Holy Spirit and the Christian life are intimately connected.

But we have yet to speak explicitly about the Triune God and of the relationships between the three persons we call Spirit, Christ, Maker; Creator, Redeemer, Sustainer; Love, Lover, Beloved. An emphasis on Hebrew thinking and on God the Spirit has perhaps tempered the christological. Yet the entire venture is incarnational, sensing the Word made flesh, Immanuel, God with us, to be Spirit, to be Creator. The anointing of Jesus, by the sages, by the women, by the Pharisee, set him apart, as priests and kings and prophets had been consecrated in Israel. Jesus the Christ, the Anointed, is the priest who offers lavish sacrifice to God for us and is himself Lavish Sacrifice. Jesus of Nazareth, God's beloved, is the Spirit-filled prophet proclaiming God's Word and is Living Word. Jesus the child born in Bethlehem, received by sages and feared by Herod as coming ruler, becomes Humble Servant, Friend of Sinners.

In a Spirit sensing system, how do we speak of the threeness and the oneness of God? In an embodied theology of Spirit, how do we speak of the three as personal, relational, yet non-hierarchical? It is easier to speak of the oneness of God who is Spirit, Creator, and Incarnate Word, than it is to speak of the three in a given order. Trinitarian theology has the immanent Trinity (Father-Son-Spirit) to speak of the relations between the three persons, yet this formula's exclusive masculinity, its hierarchical order, and the impersonality of the "third" person pose problems for a theology that views the Spirit as equal in every way to the "first" two. The so-called economic Trinity speaks of the three in terms of their primary roles or functions: Creator, Redeemer, Sustainer. Yet this formula suggests a division of labor that is too neat and hardly embracing of the numberless ways the three-personed God is active in the world. Augustine's psychological model viewed the Trinity as three different ways of saying "God is love." God is Love, Lover, and Loved. This model offers a dynamism lacking in the other two, and though it solves some of their problems, it creates new ones.

The point that Catherine LaCugna made in *God for Us* becomes crystal clear: We need more than one Trinitarian model to say what needs to be said about God's grace, redemption, and love.[6] We need to be honest about the limits of language and of formulas and models in speaking about God, yet as Christians we must find ways to profess our faith in the Triune God. As we expand the circle, the circumference of mystery is not encompassed, but grows. This Spirit-centered reflection is actually a Spirit-encompassed, a Spirit-eccentric reflection, for it would seem to me that the Spirit is the most universal of the three persons, the most ubiquitous, to use Welker's word, the most "polyconcrete," the most capable of making a home within embodied human beings while remaining utterly divine. If the Spirit is the most universal, then Christ is the most particular, so particular, in fact, that many take offense, rejecting the radical particularity of a male Jew, born of a woman, who forgave sins, and who spoke of himself as the Way, the Truth, and the Life. The three-personed God is both universal and particular—Spirit, Love, Anointed—and those of us who call ourselves Christian, who believe Jesus to be fully human and fully divine, by believing, place ourselves in a circle of vision centered on the particularity of the Incarnation, moving outward toward the one God who is Parent, Creator, Gracious Judge, and Righteous Lawgiver, toward the all-encompassing Spirit who is free and boundless but who lives with us, incarnate in our embodied particularity. This vision must also be Christo-eccentric, for the love of God in Christ must by its very nature move outward—loving, welcoming, saving, healing.[7]

By the very form of this venture, by creating a shape, shaping a genre which follows the contours of embodied life, I have tried to keep this theological exercise sensate, somatic, concrete, qualities not usually associated with the Spirit. It has been an experiment, inductive rather than deductive, based on the notion that if form and content work together dynamically to create meaning in human creations like art and music and literature and theology, then maybe that dynamic can help us understand how it is that the unbounded Spirit of God can take up residence in the created world, finding a home, a form for her activity within living, breathing beings who are quirky, fallible, and utterly particular. By her indwelling our lives are given meaning; by our welcome God's life is given meaning.

Notes

Introduction

[1]Before the advent of feminist theology, Evelyn Underhill and Georgia Harkness published significant books on the Holy Spirit: *The Golden Sequence: A Fourfold Study of the Spiritual Life* (London: Methuen, 1932) and *The Fellowship of the Holy Spirit* (Nashville: Abindgon Press, 1966), respectively.

[2]Elizabeth Johnson, *She Who Is: The Mystery of God in Feminist Theological Discourse* (New York: Crossroad, 1993) is one notable exception. Her chapter on Spirit-Sophia is expanded in her Madeleva Lecture in Spirituality, published as *Women, Earth and Creator Spirit* (New York: Paulist Press, 1993).

[3]Important recent pneumatologies include Yves Congar, *I Believe in the Holy Spirit*, 3 vols., trans. D. Smith (New York: Seabury, 1983); José Comblin, *The Holy Spirit and Liberation*, trans. Paul Burns (Maryknoll, N.Y.: Orbis Books, 1989); Jürgen Moltmann, *The Spirit of Life: A Universal Affirmation*, trans. Margaret Kohl (Minneapolis: Fortress Press, 1992); and Michael Welker, *God the Spirit*, trans. John F. Hoffmeyer (Minneapolis: Fortress Press, 1994). Chung Hyun Kyung's address at the Canberra Assembly of the World Council of Churches, "Come Holy Spirit—Renew the Whole Creation," printed in Michael Kinnamon, ed., *Signs of the Spirit: Offical Report, Seventh Assembly* (Geneva: World Council Churches, 1991), pp. 37–47, remains a kind of benchmark for feminist pneumatology.

[4]Peter Moore's essay, "Mystical Experience, Mystical Doctrine, Mystical Technique," in Steven Katz, ed., *Mysticism and Philosophical Analysis* (New York: Oxford University Press, 1978), pp. 101–131, is extremely helpful in its distinction of three orders of mystical writing: first-order autobiographical reports, second-order impersonal accounts, and third-order theological or liturgical accounts, the latter moving to more abstract reflection but bearing little reference to the concrete mystical experience itself. It seems clear that this urge toward abstraction is a function of academic training and convention.

[5]This is certainly true of male as well as female mystics. See the work of Caroline Walker Bynum, especially *The Resurrection of the Body in Western Christianity, 200–1336* (New York: Columbia University Press, 1995), and Elizabeth Alvilda Petroff, *Body and Soul: Essays on Medieval Women and Mysticism* (New York: Oxford University Press, 1994).

[6]While I do not agree fully with Joann Wolski Conn's claim, in "Toward Spiritual Maturity," that "until the High Middle Ages all theology was spiritual theology" (p. 237), I do agree that with the rise of the universities and the triumph of doctrinal genres, "'sacred science' gradually moved away from its explicit foundation in spiritual experience and focused on a foundation in philosophy, logical argumentation, or even in controversy" (p. 238). References are to Conn's chapter in Catherine Mowry LaCugna, ed., *Freeing Theology: The Essentials of Theology in Feminist Perspective* (San Francisco: HarperCollins, 1993), pp. 235–259. This resonates with a key point in Edward Farley, *Theologia: The Fragmentation and Unity of Theological Education* (Philadelphia: Fortress Press, 1983), which traces the fragmentation of theology to the Middle Ages, when *theologia* as a scholarly discipline took precedence in the academy over *theologia* as spiritual knowledge (*habitus*). See esp. ch. 2, "Theologia: The History of a Concept," pp. 29–48.

[7]In fact feminist scholars have gone so far as to note the violence done to women's bodies by the traditional eucharistic symbolism of Christian worship. See, for instance, Marjorie Procter-Smith, in *Praying With Our Eyes Open: Engendering Feminist Liturgical Prayer* (Nashville: Abingdon Press, 1995), who says, "The symbolism of bread and wine/body and blood as redemptive mystifies the real blood shed and real bodies broken in violence and abuse. Issues of body, of sin and forgiveness, of love and sacrifice, are raised in this ritual in ways that are rarely if ever nourishing to the survivor" (p.117).

[8]Some of the key books on the subject include: Grace Janzen, *The World, God's Body* (Philadelphia: Westminster Press, 1984); Sallie McFague, *The Body of God: An Ecological Theology* (Minneapolis: Fortress Press, 1993); Elizabeth Johnson, *She Who Is* (New York: Crossroad, 1993) and *Women, Earth and Creator Spirit* (New York: Paulist Press, 1993); and E. Moltmann-Wendel, *I Am My Body: A Theology of Embodiment* (New York: Continuum, 1995).

[9]Feminist theologians from Ruether to Johnson have identified dualism as a problem for Western thinking and for Christian theology in that it leads to hierarchy, especially patriarchy, or what Elisabeth Schüssler Fiorenza calls "kyriarchy," the rule of master or lord. See Elisabeth Schüssler Fiorenza, *But She Said: Feminist Practices of Biblical Interpretation* (Boston: Beacon Press, 1992), p. 117.

[10]Mary Gray, "Where Does the Wild Goose Fly To? Seeking a New Theology of the Spirit for Feminist Theology," *New Blackfriars* 72:846 (February 1991), 89–96.

[11]Johnson, *Women, Earth*, p. 17. Johnson quotes Rosemary Ruether in this context, who says, "It is perhaps not too much to say that the Achilles heel of human civilization, which today has reached global genocidal and ecocidal proportions, resides in this false development of maleness through repression of the female." Rosemary Radford Ruether, *New Woman, New Earth: Sexist Ideologies and Human Liberation* (New York: Seabury Press, 1975), p. 11, quoted by Johnson, p. 17.

[12]Johnson, p. 18.

[13]In my dissertation, "Genre, Metaphor, and Theology: The Interpretation of Form and Content in Theological Texts" (Berkeley: Graduate Theological Union, 1990), I argue that theological reflection has been done in three dynamically interconnected modes—the doctrinal, the spiritual, and the liturgical—each with its characteristic forms and genres. I maintain that spiritual and liturgical forms are *bona fide* theological reflection, overshadowed by the systematic forms, but rich resources for constructive theology. I also maintain that form matters in the interpretation of a text.

[14]Paul Ricoeur, *Interpretation Theory: Discourse and the Surplus of Meaning* (Fort Worth: Texas Christian University Press, 1976); see also *Time and Narrative*, vol. 1, trans. Kathleen McLaughlin and David Pellauer (Chicago: University of Chicago Press, 1984).

[15]Hans-Georg Gadamer, *Truth and Method*, trans. Garrett Barden and John Cumming (New York: Continuum, 1980).

[16]An excellent summary of the appeal to *phronesis* in hermeneutics may be found in Charles W. Allen, "The Primacy of *Phronesis*: A Proposal for Avoiding Frustrating Tendencies in Our Conceptions of Rationality," *The Journal of Religion* (1989) 69: 359–374 .

[17]See, for instance, Caroline Myss, *Anatomy of the Spirit: The Seven Stages of Power and Healing* (New York: Harmony Books, 1996).

Chapter 1: Spirit, Speech, Silence

[1] Isaac Watts' hymn is a paraphrase of Psalm 146.

[2] "Finding a voice," and "being heard into speech," are common themes of feminist and liberation theologians. See, for instance, Rebecca Chopp, *The Power to Speak: Feminism, Language, God* (New York: Crossroad, 1991); Susan Brooks Thistlethwaite and Mary Potter Engel, eds., *Lift Every Voice: Constructing Christian Theologies from the Underside* (San Francisco: HarperCollins, 1990); and Nelle Morton, *The Journey is Home* (Boston: Beacon Press, 1985).

[3] These words are included in the Holy Spirit section of *A Brief Statement of Faith* of the Presbyterian Church (U.S.A.), line 70. This theme is echoed in Chung Hyun Kyung's presentation at the Canberra Assembly of the World Council of Churches, "Come Holy Spirit—Renew the Whole Creation," in Michael Kinnamon, ed., *Signs of the Spirit: Official Report, Seventh Assembly* (Geneva: World Council Churches Publications, 1991), pp. 37–47. In speaking of Pentecost, Chung says, "The rush of wild wind and fire for life from God called them out from the culture of silence, violence, and death, and called them into speech, the language of their own" (p. 42).

[4] A. N. Whitehead, in *Modes of Thought* (New York: Capricorn Books, 1958), says this about human speech: "There is a deeper reason for the unconscious recourse to sound-production. Hands and arms constitute the more unnecessary parts of the body. We can do without them. They do not excite the intimacies of bodily existence. Whereas in the production of sound, the lungs and throat are brought into play. So that in speech, while a superficial, manageable expression is diffused, yet the sense of the vague intimacies of organic existence is also excited. Thus, voice-produced sound is a natural symbol for the deep experiences of organic existence" (p. 45). I agree with what he is saying about embodied speech, but I disagree that limbs are superfluous.

[5] Rebecca Goldstein, *The Mind-Body Problem* (New York: Penguin Books, 1993).

[6] See, for instance, Peter R. L. Brown, *The Body and Society: Men, Women, and Sexual Renunciation in Early Christianity* (New York: Columbia University Press, 1988); Margaret Ruth Miles, *Augustine on the Body* (Missoula, Mont.: Scholars Press, 1979); or Mary Timothy Prokes, *Toward a Theology of the Body* (Grand Rapids, Mich.: Eerdmans, 1996).

[7] Heinz Kohut, for instance, uses the phrase "independent center of initiative" to define the self in *The Restoration of the Self* (New York: International Universities Press, 1977), p. 99. Another prominent self psychologist, Joseph Lichtenberg, says "I define the self as an independent center for initiating, organizing, and integrating." See *Psychoanalysis and Motivation* (Hillsdale, N.Y.: Analytic Press, 1989), p. 12.

[8] Katherine Doob Sakenfeld, in her comments on Numbers in Carol A. Newsom and Sharon H. Ringe, eds., *The Women's Bible Commentary* (Louisville: Westminster/John Knox Press, 1992), p. 50, says of this passage, "it seems obvious that men would have sought to maintain economic control within their households…However the law is read, its ancient purpose seems to have been the promotion of family stability within a culture of male-dominated households."

[9] This translation of Psalm 63 follows that of the International Commission on English in the Liturgy in *The Psalter: A Faithful and Inclusive Rendering from the Hebrew into Contemporary English* (Chicago: Liturgy Training Publications, 1994).

Other Psalms that echo this sense of *nephesh* include Psalms 42—43, 84, and 104. Quotations from *The Psalter* will be noted.

[10]Clearly the Septuagint had an influence on the translation of these Hebrew terms into Greek, and of Hebrew anthropology as well. Reinhold Niebuhr has pointed out that *ruach* became associated with spirit or *nous*, *nephesh* with soul or *psyche*, and that Greek thinking had "dualistic consequences." See *The Nature and Destiny of Man: A Christian Interpretation* (New York: Scribners, 1946), p. 13. Earlier, he says, "The Bible knows nothing of a good mind and an evil body" (p. 7). Though Niebuhr's argument here supports my own, note should be made of the important critique feminist theologians have made of his anthropology. See Valerie Saiving Goldstein's now-classic essay, "The Human Situation: A Feminine View," in Carol P. Christ and Judith Plaskow, eds., *Womanspirit Rising: A Feminist Reader in Religion* (San Francisco: Harper and Row, 1979), pp. 25–42, and more recent writings by Susan Nelson Dunfee, "The Sin of Hiding: A Feminist Critique of Reinhold Niebuhr's Account of the Sin of Pride," *Soundings* 65, 3 (Fall 1982): 316–327, and Marjorie Suchocki, *The Fall to Violence: Original Sin in Relational Theology* (New York: Continuum, 1994).

[11]Robert Alter, *The Art of Biblical Poetry* (New York: Basic Books, 1985).

[12]*Lev* and *levav* are semantic equivalents, but favored one over the other in the varied literature of the Bible. See Francis Brown, S.R. Driver, and Charles A. Briggs, *A Hebrew and English Lexicon of the Old Testament* (Oxford: Clarendon Press, 1963), p. 523, for a summary of their usage (hereafter cited as BDB).

[13]Susan L. Nelson, *Healing the Broken Heart: Sin, Alienation and the Gift of Grace* (St. Louis: Chalice Press, 1997) borrows the notion of sin as "brokenheartedness" from Rita Nakashima Brock, *Journeys by Heart: A Christology of Erotic Power* (New York: Crossroad, 1988) who says, "To take heart is to gain courage" (xiv).

[14]BDB, p. 924

[15]BDB points out that this usage of *ruach*, as Spirit of God, does not appear in Jahwist or Deuteronomic literature (p. 925).

[16]Michael Welker, in *God the Spirit*, trans. John F. Hoffmeyer (Minneapolis: Fortress Press, 1994), offers a reading of these passages in Judges which argues that the action of God's Spirit brings about "an unexpected, unforeseeable renewal of the people's unanimity and capacity for action, a renewal of the people's power of resistance in the midst of universal despair, and a resulting change of fate" (p. 53).

[17]Christian feminists, while very clear about the patriarchy in both testaments, are rightly charged with anti-Judaism when they claim that earliest Christianity challenged and improved upon the sexist Judaism of the day. See Katherine von Kellenbach, *Anti-Judaism in Christian-Rooted Feminist Writings* (Atlanta: Scholars Press, 1994).

[18]Early Christian martyrs, those whose confession of faith resulted in death, literally bore witness with their bodies. The Hebrew root, *bsr*, which gives us the noun *basar*, flesh, sounds like the verb that means "bear tidings."

[19]Isak Dinesen, "The Blank Page," in *Last Tales* (New York: Vintage Books, 1975) pp. 99–106. This story and its central image have become paradigmatic for feminist literary criticism. See, for instance, Susan Gubar, "'The Blank Page' and the Issues of Female Creativity," in *Writing and Sexual Difference*, ed. Elizabeth Abel (Chicago: University of Chicago Press, 1981), pp. 73–94.

[20]Karen Jo Torjesen, *When Women Were Priests: Women's Leadership in the Early Church and the Scandal of their Subordination in the Rise of Christianity* (San Francisco: HarperCollins, 1993), pp. 9–10.

[21]Marguerite Porete, *The Mirror of Simple Souls,* ed. Ellen Babinsky (New York: Paulist Press, 1993).

[22]Letty Russell in *Human Liberation in a Feminist Perspective—A Theology* (Philadelphia: Westminster Press, 1974) speaks of learning from the past, through "reflection on its meaning and its mistakes," in order to build a usable future (p. 72). She cites a 1965 essay by Henry S. Commager as the source of this term, while William Bouwsma claims to get the title of his book, *A Usable Past* (Berkeley: University of California, 1990), from Nietzsche. Acknowledging his own elitism, Bouwsma likens history to a "public utility," useful, belonging to all; naturally feminists and liberation theologians are suspicious of such a view.

[23]Carol Lee Flinders, *At the Root of This Longing: Reconciling a Spiritual Hunger and a Feminist Thirst* (San Francisco: HarperCollins, 1998), p.158.

[24]Rosemary Ruether and Eleanor McLaughlin, eds., *Women of Spirit: Female Leadership in the Jewish and Christian Traditions* (New York: Simon and Schuster, 1979), pp. 19–20.

[25]Though most scholars seem to wonder whether he was indeed the editor, "The Martyrdom of Perpetua and Felicitas" is included as a kind of appendix to Tertullian's *Ad Marturas* in the *Ante-Nicene Fathers,* vol. 3, pp. 697–706. It is in his treatise, "On the Apparel of Women," that Tertullian says, "You are the devil's gateway: you are the unsealer of that forbidden tree: you are the first deserter of the divine law…you destroyed so easily God's image, man" (vol. 4, p. 14).

[26]The translation here is that of H. R. Musurillo, *The Acts of the Christian Martyrs* (Oxford: Clarendon Press, 1971). Chapter numbers refer to this edition.

[27]See Elizabeth Alvilda Petroff's introduction in *Medieval Women's Visionary Literature* (New York: Oxford University Press, 1986), p. 61, or that of Rosemary Rader in *A Lost Tradition: Women Writers of the Early Church,* ed. Patricia Wilson-Kastner, G. Ronald Kastner, Ann Millin, Rosemary Rader, and Jeremiah Reedy (Lanham, Md.: University Press of America, 1981), p. 13, n. 1.

[28]Petroff, p. 24.

[29]Hildegard of Bingen, Letter to Bernard excerpted in Emilie Zum Brunn and Georgette Epiney-Burgard, eds., *Women Mystics in Medieval Europe,* trans. Sheila Hughes (New York: Paragon House, 1989), pp. 19–21.

[30]Elisabeth of Schönau, *Visions,* in Petroff, p. 159.

[31]Walter J. Ong, *Orality and Literacy,* pp. 113–14, in Petroff, p. 31.

[32]Mechtild of Magdeburg, *The Flowing Light of the Godhead,* trans. Lucy Menzies, in Petroff, p. 212.

[33]*The Book of Margery Kempe,* trans. B. A. Windeatt (New York: Penguin Books, 1985), p. 34.

[34]Julian of Norwich, *Showings,* trans. and ed. by Edmund Colledge and James Walsh (New York: Paulist Press, 1978), p. 135.

[35]Alison Weber, *Teresa of Avila and the Rhetoric of Femininity* (Princeton: Princeton University Press, 1990), p. 29.

[36]In the Prologue to *The Interior Castle,* trans. Kieran Kavanaugh and Otilio Rodriguez (New York: Paulist Press, 1979), p. 35, Teresa claims to be writing to her sisters in "the language used between women…So, I shall be speaking to them while I write." Weber argues that she is addressing the *letrados,* the scholars of the church as well.

[37]*Interior Castle,* p. 119.

[38]Elaine C. Huber, "'A Woman Must Not Speak': Quaker Women in the English Left Wing," in *Women of Spirit,* pp. 152–181.

[39]"Womens Speaking Justified, Proved and Allowed of by the Scriptures" (London: Pythia Press, 1989), in McHaffie, *Readings in HerStory,* pp. 110–112.

[40]Robley Edward Whitson, ed., *The Shakers: Two Centuries of Spiritual Reflection* (New York: Paulist Press, 1983), p. 9.

[41]Marjorie Procter-Smith, "Shakerism and Feminism: Reflections on Women's Religion and the Early Shakers," *Shaker* (September 1991).

[42]Procter-Smith provides a helpful summary of the writings of a number of feminists who have studied the Shakers and their teachings, including Barbara Brown Zikmund, Rosemary Radford Ruether, Mary Farrell Bednarowski, and Linda Mercadente.

[43]Although I am a lifelong Presbyterian, from a long line of Presbyterians on my father's side, I discovered after joining the faculty of a seminary associated with the Christian Church (Disciples of Christ) that my mother's grandmother, Lulu Mulkey, was a direct descendent of Philip Mulkey, a Baptist preacher who, with his brother John, was an early leader in what became the Stone-Campbell movement.

[44]This and the following account are quoted by Richard L. Harrison, Jr., in *From Camp Meeting to Church: A History of the Christian Church (Disciples of Christ) in Kentucky* (St. Louis: Christian Board of Publication, 1992), p. 24.

[45]Ibid.

Chapter 2: Vision, Verdure, Viridity

[1]Miriam Therese Winter, *WomanPrayer, WomanSong: Resources for Ritual* (Philadelphia: Meyer Stone, 1987), pp. 27–8.

[2]See Catherine Mowry LaCugna, *God for Us: The Trinity and Christian Life* (San Francisco: HarperCollins, 1991).

[3]Quotations from the Psalms in this section are from *The Psalter.*

[4]Most biblical scholars divide the prophecy of Isaiah into three major sections representing at least three different contexts and authors. Isaiah 1—39 dates to the 8th century B.C.E., a time when Israel was divided and under siege from Assyria. Isaiah 40—55, or Deutero-Isaiah, dates to the latter days of the Babylonian Captivity. The final chapters (56—66), sometimes called Trito-Isaiah, address the exiles after their return to Palestine. See, for instance, Norman K. Gottwald, *The Hebrew Bible* (Philadelphia: Fortress Press, 1985), pp. 377–387, 492–502.

[5]Hildegard of Bingen, *Scivias*, trans. Mother Columba Hart and Jane Bishop (New York: Paulist Press, 1990), pp. 344–346. Page numbers refer to this edition.

[6]Hildegard of Bingen, *The Book of the Rewards of Life*, trans Bruce W. Hozeski (New York: Oxford University Press, 1994). Page numbers refer to this edition.

[7]In the Sixth Part, the four elements come into play (pp. 271–273). Air, fire, and water appeal to the senses of sound, touch, and taste.

[8]Julian of Norwich, *Showings*, trans. Edmund Colledge and James Walsh (New York: Paulist Press, 1978). Page numbers refer to this edition.

[9]Julian would have lived by some version of the *Ancrene Wisse* or *Riwle*. See *Anchoritic Spirituality*, trans. Anne Savage and Nicholas Watson (New York: Paulist Press, 1991), for history and examples of such rules.

[10]Augustine, in *De Trinitate*, Books 9–10, sets forth his "psychological" trinity, with the formulation Lover, Beloved, and Love for the three persons.

[11]In the critical edition, *A Book of Showings to the Anchoress Julian of Norwich* (Toronto: Pontifical Institute of Mediaeval Studies, 1978), Colledge and Walsh cite a number of biblical and literary references to "*the grett root.*" See p. 542, n. 300.

[12]A sampling includes, Christopher Bamford and William Parker Marsh, eds., *Celtic Christianity: Ecology and Holiness* (Edinburgh: Floris Books, 1982); Esther de Waal, ed., *The Celtic Vision: Prayers and Blessings from the Outer Hebrides* (London:

Darton, Longman, and Todd, 1988); Shirley Toulson, *The Celtic Year: A Month-by-Month Celebration of Celtic Christian Festivals and Sites* (Rockport, Mass.: Element, 1993); Edward C. Sellner, *Wisdom of the Celtic Saints* (South Bend, Ind.: Ave Maria Press, 1993); and J. Philip Newell, *Celtic Prayers from Iona* (New York: Paulist Press, 1997).

[13]Oliver Davies and Fiona Bowie, eds, *Celtic Christian Spirituality: An Anthology of Medieval and Modern Sources* (New York: Continuum, 1995), p. 20.

[14]Attributed to Ciaran of Clonmacnois, *Litany of Confession*, in Davies and Bowie, p. 45.

[15]Alexander Carmichael, *Carmina Gadelica: Hymns and Incantations Collected in the Highlands and Islands of Scotland in the Last Century* (Edinburgh: Lindisfarne Press, 1992).

[16]Fedja Anzelewsky, *Dürer: His Art and Life*, trans. Heide Grieve (Freiburg: Office du Livre, 1980). Of "The Large Piece of Turf," Anzelewsky says, "He appears to have been conscious of the fact that no painter before him had dared to represent such an insignificant piece of nature…this picture expresses the artist's awe at the beauty of even such an insignificant part of God's creation" (p. 108).This art is on the cover of this book.

[17]John Calvin, *Institutes of the Christian Religion*, ed. John McNeill, trans. Ford Lewis Battles (Philadelphia: Westminster Press, 1960), Book I, Chapter xi, Section 4. Quoted material is from this edition; references are to Book, Chapter, Section.

[18]Peter Gay, *The Enlightenment: An Interpretation—The Rise of Modern Paganism* (New York: W. W. Norton, 1966).

[19]Alfred, Lord Tennyson, "In Memoriam A. H. H.," v. 59. The poem was written in 1833.

[20]William Wordsworth, "The Tables Turned," 1798, lines 9–12, 21–24.

[21]Samuel Taylor Coleridge, *Biographia Literaria*, 2 vols. (Oxford Reprint of 1817 edition), 1:202.

[22]Samuel Taylor Coleridge, *Confessions of an Inquiring Spirit*, ed. H. StJ. Hart (Stanford, Calif.: Stanford University Press, 1967). Page numbers cited are from this edition.

[23]Coleridge and Schleiermacher were contemporaries; it is not known whether they met or were directly influenced by one another, though their hermeneutics, in particular, reflect a number of parallels, both being grounded in Kant and influenced by German Romanticism. A number of intriguing essays on the two appear in David Jasper, ed., *The Interpretation of Belief: Coleridge, Schleiermacher and Romanticism* (New York: St. Martin's Press, 1986). See especially Stephen Prickett, "On Reading Nature as a Romantic," pp. 126–142.

[24]Hildegard, *Scivias*, p. 47.

[25]Ibid., p.53.

[26]Matthew Fox, *Original Blessing: A Primer in Creation Spirituality* (Santa Fe, N.M.: Bear and Co., 1983).

[27]See, for instance, *Creation Spirituality: Liberating Gifts for the Peoples of the Earth* (San Francisco: HarperCollins, 1991).

[28]Rosemary Radford Ruether, "Motherearth and the Megamachine: A Theology of Liberation in a Feminine, Somatic and Ecological Perspective," in Carol P. Christ and Judith Plaskow, eds, *Womanspirit Rising: A Feminist Reader in Religion* (San Francisco: Harper and Row, 1978), pp. 43–52. The essay first appeared in 1972. Pages cited in these two paragraphs are from this essay.

[29]Important work has been done in this area, notably Rosemary Radford Ruether, *Gaia and God: An Ecofeminist Theology of Earth Healing* (San Francisco: HarperCollins, 1991); Sallie McFague, *The Body of God: An Ecological Theology* (Minneapolis: Fortress Press, 1993); Anne Primavesi, *From Apocalypse to Genesis: Ecology, Feminism, and Christianity* (Minneapolis: Fortress Press, 1991), and McFague, *Super, Natural Christians: How We Should Love Nature* (Minneapolis: Fortress Press, 1997).

[30]Grace Janzen, in *God's World, God's Body* (Philadelphia: Westminster Press, 1984), traces a more holistic view of soul and body through Hebrew scripture and Christian tradition, concluding that "a Christian doctrine of persons requires, in its key affirmations of creation, sin, salvation, and the future state, an anthropology which accepts the body as an aspect of total personhood. Radical dualism and a denigration of the physical is not an option for Christian theology" (p. 9).

[31]Anne Primavesi, in her article on "Pantheism" in Letty M. Russell and J. Shannon Clarkson, eds., *Dictionary of Feminist Theologies* (Louisville: Westminster John Knox, 1996), pp. 199–200, notes that feminist theologians share a resistance to pantheism with traditional Christianity. This reference work is cited hereafter as *DFT*.

[32]Ewert Cousins, ed., *Process Theology* (New York: Newman Press, 1971), p. 14. I like Sallie McFague's definition of panentheism: "A panentheistic view of the relation of God and the world is compatible with our model of God as the spirit that is the source, the life, the breath of all reality. Everything that is is *in* God and God is *in* all things and yet God is not identical with the universe, for the universe is dependent on God in a way that God is not dependent on the universe" (*The Body of God*, p. 149).

[33]Suchocki, *Fall to Violence*, p. 48.

[34]Annie Dillard, *Pilgrim at Tinker Creek* (New York: Harper and Row, 1974), p. 30.

Chapter 3: Desire, Denial, Delight

[1]No one in the Prichard family knows for sure who wrote this blessing, though some believe that my great-grandfather, Augustus Bedlow Prichard, a Presbyterian minister, wrote it. I recently discovered that its tune is an American folk-hymn called "Greenfields."

[2]Note the connection between the Canticle of Mary and that of Hannah in 1 Samuel 2:1–10. There are other parallels including Psalm 107:9: "[God] satisfies the thirsty, and the hungry [God] fills with good things."

[3]Roberta Bondi, *To Pray and to Love: Conversations on Prayer with the Early Church* (Minneapolis: Fortress Press, 1991), p. 119.

[4]Though fathers predominated, there were women who went to the desert to pray, who formed spiritual communities, and whose sayings are preserved. See Andrew Kadel, *Matrology: A Bibliography of Writings by Christian Women from the First to the Fifteenth Century* (New York: Continuum, 1995), pp. 142–44; and Ross S. Kraemer, ed., *Maenads, Martyrs, Matrons, Monastics: A Sourcebook on Women's Religions in the Greco-Roman World* (Philadelphia: Fortress Press, 1988), pp. 117–124.

[5]Teresa M. Shaw, *The Burden of the Flesh: Fasting and Sexuality in Early Christianity* (Minneapolis: Fortress Press, 1998). As a *magistra*, we can hardly call her book magisterial.

[6]Ibid., p. 6. Shaw argues for the connections between fasting and bodily health, noting that abstinence from food and sex were connected in the practice of early ascetics.

[7]Derwas J. Chitty, *The Desert a City: An Introduction to the Study of Egyptian and Palestinian Monasticism under the Christian Empire* (Crestwood, N.Y.: St. Vladimir's Seminary Press, 1966), pp. 5–7.

[8]Athanasius, *The Life of Antony and the Letter to Marcellinus*, trans. Robert C. Gregg (New York: Paulist Press, 1980).

[9]Athanasius tells of Antony entering a church and hearing the gospel reading, Jesus' words to the rich man (Mt. 19:21), as "if the passage were read on his account" (p. 31), and immediately doing likewise.

[10]Chitty, p. 5.

[11]Ibid., p. 67.

[12]These sayings are available in a number of anthologies and editions including Benedicta Ward, ed., *The Wisdom of the Desert Fathers* (Oxford: SLG Press, 1986); Thomas Merton, trans., *The Wisdom of the Desert: Some Sayings of the Desert Fathers* (Norfolk, Conn.: New Directions, 1960); and Owen Chadwick, ed., *Western Asceticism* (Philadelphia: The Westminister Press, 1958), pp. 33–189. Three Ammas are named in the *Apophthegmata*, Sarah, Syncletica, and Theodora; see Kraemer, ed., *Maenads*, pp. 117–124. Citations in this section refer to one of these four editions.

[13]Kraemer, p. 118.

[14]Ibid., p. 120.

[15]Chadwick, p. 49.

[16]Merton, p. 77.

[17]Ward p. 5.

[18]Merton, p. 74.

[19]Kraemer, p. 117.

[20]Ward, p. 18.

[21]Chadwick, p. 58.

[22]Ward, p. 14.

[23]Merton, p. 49. Mary Daly calls this flight a kind of "sadospirituality...phallic flight from lust into lust-full asceticism." *Pure Lust: Elemental Feminist Philosophy* (Boston: Beacon Press, 1984), p. 72.

[24]Note that Shaw sees this view as being read into the desert spirituality from a later perspective: "For all of the rhetorical condemnations of the flesh in ascetic literature, the steady, intent focus on the appearance of the body as a sign of holiness and sanctification refutes any easy dismissal of asceticism as bizarre or dualistic" (p. 21).

[25]*Life of Antony*, ch. 14, p. 42.

[26]Chitty, p. 4. *Life of Antony*, ch. 92, p. 98.

[27]Placid Spearritt, "Benedict," in Cheslyn Jones, Geoffrey Wainwright, and Edward Yarnold, eds., *The Study of Spirituality* (New York: Oxford Univerity Press, 1986), pp. 148–156.

[28]Carolyn Walker Bynum, *Holy Feast and Holy Fast: The Religious Significance of Food to Medieval Women* (Berkeley: University of California Press, 1987).

[29]Cyprian, Letter 62 *(To Caecilius)*, quoted in James F. White, *Documents of Christian Worship: Descriptive and Interpretive Sources* (Louisville: Westminster/John Knox Press, 1992), pp. 188–89. Cyprian's words echo early communion prayers, including that of the *Didache*: "As this piece [of bread] was scattered over the hills and then was brought together and made one, so let your Church be brought together from the ends of the earth into your Kingdom," quoted in White, p. 182.

[30]Bynum, *Holy Feast*, p. 33. While some early prayers do speak of the bread and wine as Christ's broken body and shed blood, the suffering of Christ appears less pivotal than the unity of the body. See, for instance, Hippolytus, *The Apostolic*

Tradition, in R.C.D. Jasper and G. J. Cuming, eds., *Prayers of the Eucharist: Early and Reformed* (New York: Oxford University Press, 1980), pp. 22–25.

[31]Bynum, *Holy Feast*, p. 59.

[32]Ibid., p. 60.

[33]Ibid., pp. 59–60.

[34]In a study concurrent with Bynum's, Rudoph M. Bell considers the connections between medieval and contemporary women who have literally lost their appetites. See *Holy Anorexia* (Chicago: University of Chicago Press, 1985).

[35]Nuptial imagery derived from the Song of Songs will be considered more fully in chapter 5.

[36]Bynum, *Holy Feast*, p. 69, claims that "both feast and fast were more central to women's spirituality than to men's." Rudolph Bell seeks to persuade those interested in the history of women "that a historically significant group of women exhibited an anorexic behavior pattern in response to the patriarchal social structures in which they were trapped" (xii).

[37]Catherine of Siena is one of only two women, with Teresa of Avila, to have been named "Doctor of the Church." Her text, *The Dialogue*, translated by Suzanne Noffke, O.P. (New York: Paulist Press, 1980) will serve as primary source for this section.

[38]Catherine uses imagery of breast-feeding in various ways throughout the *Dialogue*. Jesus is our wet nurse, who takes the bitter medicine of death "so that he might heal and give life to you who were babies weakened by sin" (p. 52). The perverse priests, who feed at the breasts of mother church, she says, "ought not only to feed themselves, but hold to those breasts the whole body of Christianity" (p. 50).

[39]"Divine Providence," esp. pp. 277–296.

[40]For further elaboration on the shifts in piety and charity see Rebecca Button Prichard, "Health, Education, and Welfare in the Protestant Reformation: Who Cared?" *Encounter* (Fall 1994).

[41]John Calvin, *Institutes*, Book III, offers a lengthy critique of medieval penance, holding fast to the Protestant notion that repentance and good works are the result, not the cause of faith and salvation. In III.ii.1, Calvin begins a pivotal description of the Christian life and of self-denial which begin with God's claim on the believer and manifest in charity and love toward neighbor.

[42]IV.xii.15–28. "Christ deems marriage worthy of such honor that he wills it to be an image of his sacred union with the church [Eph. 5:23–24, 32]. What more splendid commendation could be spoken of the dignity of marriage? With what shamelessness will that be called unclean or defiled in which a likeness of Christ's spiritual grace shines forth!" (IV.xii.24)

[43]For a summary of the history of women in the Reformed tradition see Rebecca Button Prichard, "*Grandes Dames, Femmes Fortes*, and *Matrones*: Reformed Women Ministering," in Catherine Wessinger, ed., *Religious Institutions and Women's Leadership: New Roles Inside the Mainstream* (Columbia, S.C.: University of South Carolina Press, 1996), pp. 39–57.

[44]Mystics like Catherine and Teresa were certainly involved in social reform, as were Catholic women of our own century, notably Dorothy Day.

[45]Linda A. Mercadente suggests a connection between the theology of sin and human nature and attitudes toward alcoholism and addiction. See "Sin, Addiction, and Freedom," in Rebecca S. Chopp and Mark Lewis Taylor, eds., *Reconstructing Christian Theology* (Minneapolis: Fortress Press, 1994), pp. 220–244.

[46]In a recent essay, L. Gregory Jones argues that violence is the result of desire: "We desire what we cannot have, and we want to have it. Our acquisitive desire leads

us into violence." "Roots of Violence," *The Christian Century* (July 15–22, 1998), p. 692.

[47]Barbara Leslie Epstein, *The Politics of Domesticity: Women, Evangelism, and Temperance in Nineteenth-Century America* (Middletown, Conn.: Wesleyan University Press, 1981), p. 89.

[48]Ibid., p.114.

[49]Frances Willard, quoted in Epstein, p. 137.

[50]Frances Willard, *How to Win: A Book for Girls,* quoted in Rosemary Radford Ruether and Rosemary Skinner Keller, eds., *In Our Own Voices: Four Centuries of American Women's Religious Writing* (San Francisco: HarperCollins, 1995), pp. 280–281.

[51]Difference as a positive value is taught in books such as Nancy Chodorow, *The Reproduction of Mothering* (Berkeley: University of California Press, 1978), Carol Gilligan, *In a Different Voice: Psychological Theory and Women's Development* (Cambridge, Mass.: Harvard University Press, 1982); and Mary Field Belenky, Blythe McVicker Clinchy, Nancy Rule Goldberger, and Jill Mattuck Tarule, *Women's Ways of Knowing: The Development of Self, Voice, and Mind* (New York: Basic Books, 1986).

[52]Some of the French feminists argue that femininity is a male construct, so Luce Irigaray, who suggests that male culture only oppresses women, giving them a "quasi-monopoly of masochistic pleasure, housework, and reproduction." "The Sex Which is Not One," in Elaine Marks and Isabelle de Courtivron, *New French Feminisms: An Anthology* (New York: Schocken Books, 1987, 1), p. 105.

[53]Karen Baker-Fletcher, s.v. "Difference," in *DFT*, p. 68.

[54]Letty Russell, *The Future of Partnership* (Philadelphia: Westminster Press, 1979), p. 18. Over the years Russell has developed this idea of "partnership," extending it to all sorts of difference. "Diversity," she says, "is not just an ecumenical slogan that is often contradicted by our largely homogenous church communities. It represents a description of the differences of race, culture, gender, sexual orientation, age, abilities, economic and political status, and much more that are part of the world in which we live." *Church in the Round: Feminist Interpretation of the Church* (Louisville: Westminster/John Knox Press, 1993), p. 158.

[55]Johnson, *She Who Is*, p. 128.

[56]Ibid., p. 130.

[57]Sarah Coakley, "'Femininity' and the Holy Spirit," in Monica Furlong, ed., *Mirror to the Church: Reflections on Sexism* (London: SPCK, 1988), pp. 124–135.

[58]Ibid., p. 132.

[59]Isak Dinesen, *Anecdotes of Destiny and Ehrengard* (New York: Vintage Books, 1985), pp. 23–68.

Chapter 4: Feeling, Fire, Fervor

[1]Julian, *Showings*, ch. iv (short text).

[2]The Oakland hills fire is recounted by survivors in Patricia Adler, et al., eds., *Fire in the Hills: A Collective Remembrance* (Berkeley: By the Author, 1992).

[3]The Torah is full of instructions about this sacrificial system. Exodus speaks of an offering of fire to the Lord, with its pleasing odor, some 32 times (Ex. 29:18). See BDB, pp. 77–78.

[4]Joshua R. Porter, s.v. "Tabernacle," in Paul J. Achtemeier, ed., *Harper's Bible Dictionary* (San Francisco: Harper and Row, 1985), pp. 1013–14 (hereafter *HBD*), suggests that the priestly tradition "retrojected" the description of the temple back

into the tabernacle, which likely was not as elaborate as suggested in Exodus. The tent of meeting (*ohel mo'ed*) was a tent suited to bedouin existence, where the cloud hovered and where Moses "met" with God. The tent was on the edge of the camp, the tabernacle in the center, in the vicinity of the Levites.

[5]I hope to acknowledge and to avoid a supersessioinist reading of this passage. For an instructive and helpful reading see Michael E. Lodahl, *Shekhinah/Spirit: Divine Presence in Jewish and Christian Religion* (New York: Paulist Press, 1992), pp.17–21. Lodahl argues that Paul's reading of Exodus is skewed by his eschatological convictions.

[6]Lodahl points to the Targums as the first instance of the term (see p. 51, n. 20); *HBD*, p. 938, says Philo uses the term but gives no reference.

[7]Lodahl summarizes this well (p. 52) and his summary concurs with *HBD* (p. 936).

[8]Jürgen Moltmann, in *The Spirit of Life: A Universal Affirmation*, trans. Margaret Kohl (Minneapolis: Fortress Press, 1992), speaks of the Shekhinah (pp. 47–51) as God's presence without equating her to the Holy Spirit. Moltmann reads the term *Shekinah* as though it is a biblical word rather than a rabbinic derivative.

[9]Lodahl, p. 56.

[10]Lawrence Fine in Barry W. Holtz, ed., *Back to the Sources: Reading the Classic Jewish Texts* (New York: Summit Books, 1984) cites the *Sefer ha-Bahir*, which appeared in Provence in the late twelfth century, as the source for the ten Sefirot.

[11]Daniel Matt, *The Essential Kabbalah: The Heart of Jewish Mysticism* (San Francisco: HarperCollins, 1996), p. 10. For a provocative but somewhat unorthodox reading of this tradition see Caroline Myss, *Anatomy of the Spirit*, who compares the sefirot with the seven chakras of Hinduism and the seven sacraments of Christianity.

[12]Both Lodahl (pp. 93–97) and Matt (pp. 13–15) offer surveys of Luria's contribution. They both rely on Gershom Scholem, *Major Trends in Jewish Mysticism* (New York: Schocken Books, 1941), pp. 244–286.

[13]Scholem, pp. 260-261.

[14]The notion of *shevirath* is much more complicated than this. Scholem offers a detailed analysis on pp. 265–268.

[15]Matt, p. 15.

[16]Israel Sarug, *Limmudei Atsilut* (16th-17th century), quoted in Matt, p. 97.

[17]Lodahl, p. 67.

[18]Ibid., p. 72.

[19]Johnson, *She Who Is*, p. 131.

[20]The *Apostolic Tradition* of Hippolytus (26.18) attests to the connections between the Christian blessing of the light and the Jewish blessing of the lamp on the eve of the Sabbath. See Peter G. Cobb, "The History of the Christian Year," in Cheslyn Jones, Geoffrey Wainwright, and Edward Yarnold, eds., *The Study of Liturgy* (New York: Oxford University Press, 1978), p. 410; and J. D. Crichton, s.v. "New Fire," in J. G. Davies, ed., *The New Westminster Dictionary of Liturgy and Worship* (Philadelphia: The Westminster Press, 1986), p. 388 (hereafter *DLW*).

[21]Cited in Edward Foley, *From Age to Age: How Christians Celebrated the Eucharist* (Chicago: Liturgy Training Publications, 1991), p. 28.

[22]Hugh Wybrew, "Ceremonial," in Jones, et al., p. 433. See also C. E. Pocknee and G. D. W. Randall, s.v. "Candles, Lamps and Lights," in *DLW*, pp. 137–139.

[23]*Egeria: Diary of a Pilgrimage*, trans. George E. Gingras, Ancient Christian Writers, No. 38 (New York: Newman Press, 1970). This text, written by a woman on pilgrimage to the Holy Land in the fourth or fifth century, provides some of the

earliest details of the Jerusalem liturgy. In chapter 24 she describes a daily vigil at the Anastasis, or grotto of the Resurrection, and in chapter 38 describes portions of the vigil on Holy Saturday.

²⁴Both Crichton in *DLW*, p. 388, and Cobb in Jones, et al, p. 410, note the association of this ritual with St. Patrick.

²⁵According to Gingras, in the Introduction to *Egeria*, p. 39, the *Exultet* is found in a fifth-century Armenian lectionary. The full text of the *Exultet* is quoted by Ann Patrick Ware, "The Easter Vigil: A Theological and Liturgical Critique," in Marjorie Procter-Smith and Janet R. Walton, eds., *Women at Worship: Interpretations of North American Diversity* (Louisville: Westminster/John Knox Press, 1993), pp. 83–106. Ware raises serious criticisms of current Roman Catholic practice in the Easter Vigil both in its masculinism and its anti-Judaism which apply also to Anglican and Protestant revivals of the service.

²⁶Crichton, *DLW*, pp. 388–389.

²⁷Moltmann, p. 64.

²⁸Hildegard, *Scivias*, p. 59.

²⁹Hildegard's vision of the Trinity is recounted and interpreted in *Scivias*, Vision Two, p. 161.

³⁰Ibid., pp. 163–164.

³¹See the Introduction to Mechtild of Magdeburg: *The Flowing Light of the Godhead*, trans. Frank Tobin (New York: Paulist Press, 1997), pp. 1–3 (Book and chapter citations in this section are to this version). See also Fiona Bowie, ed., *Beguine Spirituality: An Anthology*, trans. Oliver Davies (London: SPCK, 1989). Bowie writes: "As the Church became increasingly paranoid concerning the presence of heterodox teachings, and brutal in its attempts to eradicate those it conceived of as a threat, beguines and beghards, along with Jews, witches and various other sects, found themselves vulnerable and subject to frequent accusations of heresy, with often terrible consequences" (p. 20).

³²This is Tobin's term in the Introduction to Mechtild, p. 17.

³³Tobin notes the literary style of Mechtild's text and the variety of forms it takes: "In her search for suitable forms she ranges far and wide, employing most genres available to an author of her time" (p. 10).

³⁴Karen Armstrong, *A History of God: The 4000-Year Quest of Judaism, Christianity and Islam* (New York: Alfred A. Knopf, 1994), p. 256.

³⁵Bengt Hoffman, *Luther and the Mystics* (Minneapolis: Augsburg, 1976), p. 18.

³⁶The original title page of Calvin's work reads as follows: "The Institutes of the Christian Religion, Containing almost the Whole Sum of Piety and Whatever It is Necessary to Know in the Doctrine of Salvation. A Work Very Well Worth Reading by All Persons Zealous for Piety, and Lately Published. A Preface to the Most Christian King of Frances, in Which this Book is Presented to Him as a Confession of Faith. Author, John Calvin, of Noyon. Basel. MCXXXVI."

³⁷The footnote here (p. 540, n. 6) gives the Latin: "*Corda nostra incendit amore Dei et studio pietatis,*" and tells us that Calvin's emblem was a flaming heart on an outstretched hand with the motto "*Cor meum quasi immolatum tibi offero, Domine.*" The note also quotes Luther as saying that faith sets the heart aflame, and it mentions Wesley's heart-warming experience as well.

³⁸See Dennis E. Tamburello, *Union with Christ: John Calvin and the Mysticism of St. Bernard* (Louisville: Westminster/John Knox Press, 1994).

³⁹Nicolas Ludwig, Count von Zinzendorf, from "Nine Public Lectures," in Peter C. Erb, ed., *Pietists: Selected Writings* (New York: Paulist Press, 1983), pp. 308–309.

[40]Ibid., p. 318. Peter C. Erb, p. 22, also notes that Zinzendorf spoke of the Trinity in familial terms, Father, Mother (Holy Spirit), and Son.

[41]John Wesley, *Journal*, May 24, 1738.

[42]Keith W. Clements, in the Introduction to *Friedrich Schleiermacher: Pioneer of Modern Theology* (Minneapolis: Fortress Press, 1991), pp. 15–17, outlines briefly the influence of the Moravians on the young Schleiermacher.

[43]Fiona Bowie, ed., *Beguine Spirituality: An Anthology* (London: SPCK, 1989), pp. 34–37.

[44]Heinrich Kraemer and Jacob Sprenger, *Malleus Maleficarum*, trans. Montague Summers (New York: Dover, 1971), pp. 44–47.

[45]Alister E. McGrath, in *A Life of John Calvin* (Oxford: Blackwell, 1990), pp. 114–120, offers a detailed account of "The Servetus Affair." He notes the widespread use of capital punishment throughout Early Modern Europe and the fact that "Servetus was the *only* individual put to death for his religious opinions in Geneva during Calvin's lifetime, at a time when executions of this nature were a commonplace elsewhere" (p. 116). Among Servetus' contemporaries, McGrath notes the execution by the Inquisition of Etienne LeCourt in Rouen for a variety of heresies including the suggestion that "women will preach the gospel" (p. 12).

[46]In a recent article by Thomas Brady and Arthur Quinn, the authors argue that the Inquisition has become a powerful myth with its origin "in historic European enmities for Roman Catholicism [and]…a merger of anti-Catholic feelings in Protestant England and Holland with anti-clerical feelings in France and Spain" (p. 19). "The Myth of the Inquisition," *California Monthly* (April 1997): 18–19.

[47]Anne Llewellyn Barstow, *Witchcraze: A New History of the European Witch Hunts— Our Legacy of Violence Against Women* (San Francisco: HarperCollins, 1994), pp. 1–2.

[48]Ibid., p. 94.

[49]Ibid., pp. 143–145.

[50]Ibid., p. 156.

[51]Michael Welker, *God the Spirit*, trans. John F. Hoffmeyer (Minneapolis: Fortress Press, 1994), p. 8. Welker cites a number of sources including D. B. Barrett, ed., *World Christian Encyclopedia: A Comparative Survey of Churches and Religions in the Modern World AD 1900-2000* (Oxford: Oxford University Press, 1982) and Barrett's updates in the journal, *AD 2000 Together*, which document phenomenal numerical growth, as much as 19 million members a year worldwide.

[52]Nancy A. Hardesty, "Evangelical Women," in Ruether and Keller, eds., *In Our Own Voices*, pp. 207–221. An account of Osman's experience is documented on pp. 234–236.

[53]Hardesty, p. 214.

[54]Bryan Wilson, "New Images of Christian Community," in John McManners, ed., *The Oxford History of Christianity* (Oxford: Oxford University Press, 1993), pp. 600f. Donald W. Dayton in *Theological Roots of Pentecostalism* (Grand Rapids: Zondervan, 1987), traces the roots of Pentecostalism within the Wesleyan Holiness movement. Catherine L. Albanese and Stephen J. Stein use the word *protopentecostalism* in their Preface to William L. Andrews, ed., *Sisters of the Spirit: Three Black Women's Autobiographies of the Nineteenth Century* (Bloomington: Indiana University Press, 1986). The texts of African Methodist Episcopal women, Jarena Lee, Zilpha Elaw, and Julia Foote are included.

[55]Hardesty, "Evangelical Women."

[56]Barbara Brown Zikmund, Adair T. Lummis, Patricia Mei Yin Chang, *Clergy Women: An Uphill Calling* (Louisville: Westminster John Knox Press, 1998), p. 13.

Zikmund et al. also describe the numerical decline of ordained women in these churches.

[57]Moltmann, p. 180.

[58]Welker, p. 271.

[59]Chung Hyun Kyung, "Come, Holy Spirit," in Kinnamon, ed., *Signs of the Spirit*, pp. 37–47.

[60]"Celebration in Zimbabwe—Ecumenical Decade: Churches in Solidarity with Women," *Horizons* (November/December 1998), pp. 24–25.

[61]Chung, in Kinnamon, ed., p. 39.

[62]Harriet Lerner, in *The Dance of Anger: A Woman's Guide to Changing the Patterns of Intimate Relationships* (New York: HarperCollins, 1985), speaks clearly about the fear of women's anger, our own fear and that of others: "Why are angry women so threatening to others? If we are guilty, depressed or self-doubting, we stay in place...angry women may change and challenge the lives of us all, as witnessed by the past decade of feminism" (p. 3). See also, Ellen Bass, *The Courage to Heal: A Guide for Women Survivors of Child Sexual Abuse* (New York: Harper and Row, 1988), especially the chapter "Anger—the Backbone of Healing," which begins, "Few women have wholeheartedly embraced anger as a positive healing force...most religious or spiritual ideologies encourage us to forgive and love. As a result, many survivors have suppressed their anger, turning it inward" (p. 122).

[63]Marjorie Hewitt Suchocki, *God-Christ-Church: A Practical Guide to Process Theology* (New York: Crossroad, 1982), p. 177.

[64]Ibid., p. 186.

Chapter 5: Aroma, Odor, Adoration

[1]Diane Ackerman, *A Natural History of the Senses* (New York: Random House, 1990), p. 37.

[2]Ibid., p. 9.

[3]Ariel Bloch and Chana Bloch, *The Song of Songs: A New Translation* (Berkeley: University of California Press, 1995). The Afterword is by Robert Alter.

[4]Ibid., p. 11.

[5]Ibid., p. 14.

[6]Bloch and Bloch relate the problematic nature of much allegorical interpretation of the Song by Jewish, Christian, and classical writers (p. 29ff). "The Song fared better," they write, "at the hands of the mystics, Jewish and Christian, who honored its literal meaning as symbolic of the human longing for union with God" (p. 32).

[7]J. Cheryl Exum and Johanna W. H. Bos, eds., "Reasoning with the Foxes: Female Wit in a World of Male Power," *Semeia* 42 (1988). This volume is devoted to women in Ancient Near Eastern texts, including biblical women, who, "Because of their subordinate status...frequently rely on indirect means to accomplish their goals; deception and trickery often feature significantly in their stories" (Preface). See also, Phyllis Bird "The Harlot as Heroine: Narrative Art and Social Presupposition in Three Old Testament Texts" *Semeia* 46 (1989): 119–140.

[8]Sallie McFague, *Metaphorical Theology: Models of God in Religious Language* (Philadelphia: Fortress Press, 1982). pp. 147–48.

[9]Ibid., p. 153. In this 1982 book, McFague identifies herself as a reforming rather than a radical or revolutionary feminist, yet she argues that both perspectives are needed. Her claim that Jesus is linked with this new root metaphor, "a new quality

of relationship" (p. 108), seems a bit supersessionist, suggesting that Jesus overcame the patriarchalism of his Jewish roots.

¹⁰Myrrh mixed with wine was meant to have a drug-like effect; Matthew says the wine is mixed with *choleh*, gall. Sour wine or vinegar is *oxos*.

¹¹Geoffrey Wainwright, *Doxology: The Praise of God in Worship, Doctrine, and Life* (Oxford: Oxford University Press, 1980), p. 364.

¹²Ibid.

¹³Lietzmann, *Messe und Herrenmahl* (Bonn, 1926), quoted in Bard Thompson, *Liturgies of the Western Church* (Philadelphia: Fortress Press, 1961), p. 15. Thompson offers excerpts of Hippolytus in this collection, pp. 20–24, as does James F. White in *Documents of Christian Worship: Descriptive and Interpretive Sources* (Louisville: Westminster/John Knox Press, 1992). References to Hippolytus' *Apostolic Tradition* will be to one of these two collections.

¹⁴Thompson, p. 21. J. D. Crichton, s.v. "Unction," in *DLW* takes this as evidence that the sick were to drink medicinal oil as well as being anointed with it. Note that Calvin makes much of the threefold office of Christ as "prophet, priest and king" (*Institutes*, II, v).

¹⁵The baptismal service is described in detail in chs. XV–XXI, included in White, pp. 151–156.

¹⁶The initiate enters the water naked. In another third-century document, the *Didascalia Apostolorum*, female initiates are to be instructed, accompanied, anointed, and baptized by female deacons, though "a man [is to] pronounce over them the invocation of the divine Names in the water" (White, p. 156). There was likely some resistance to the ministry of women, since a justification is included: "For this cause we say that the ministry of a woman deacon is especially needful and important. For our Lord and Saviour also was ministered unto by women."

¹⁷Cyril of Jerusalem, *Catechetical Lectures*, in White, p. 157.

¹⁸Two articles in *DLW* help recount these developments: s.v. "Confirmation," by E. C. Whitaker, and s.v. "Unction.," by J. D. Crichton.

¹⁹Serapion of Thmuis, *Prayer-Book*, in White, p. 222. See also Crichton, "Unction."

²⁰*Institutes*, IV, xix, 21.

²¹White, p. 224, cites documents of Vatican II which now call this sacrament "anointing of the sick." *The Book of Common Worship* of the Presbyterian Church (USA), 1993, contains baptismal rites that allow for anointing, services for wholeness which include anointing with oil, and pastoral liturgies which offer anointing and communion to those facing death.

²²E. Ann Matter, *The Voice of My Beloved: The Song of Songs in Western Medieval Christianity* (Philadelphia: University of Pennsylvania Press, 1990).

²³Alter, who collaborated with Bloch and Bloch in the work cited above, says in *The Art of Biblical Poetry* (New York: Basic Books, 1985), "the Song of Songs is the only surviving instance of purely secular love poetry from ancient Israel" (p. 185).

²⁴Matter, p. 32.

²⁵*Commentary* I, quoted in Matter, p. 30.

²⁶Ibid., p. 10, cf. pp. 60–1.

²⁷Not only does Ecclesia supplant Israel as the divine spouse in the Christian allegory, but illuminated manuscripts show Christ and Ecclesia stamping on Synagoga. See Matter, p. 93, plate 4.

²⁸Matter, p. 125.

[29]Matter seems to think that the written *Sermons* began with a series of talks to the community in Clairvaux. See pp. 123–124.

[30]Matter, ch. 6.

[31]The wounds of Christ are often likened to breasts, less often to the female genitals. "Suck not so much the wounds as the breasts of the Crucified," says Bernard in a letter quoted by Carolyn Walker Bynum in *Jesus as Mother: Studies in the Spirituality of the High Middle Ages* (Berkeley: University of California Press, 1982), p. 117. Wolfgang Riehle, *The Middle English Mystics* (London: Routledge and Kegan Paul, 1981), p. 46, cites the Franciscan, James of Milan, who in his *Stimulus Amoris* proposes "a typical and quite consciously intended analogy between this wound of Christ and the female pudenda: the *vulva*, as the place of sexual ecstasy, has, so to speak, been transformed into the *vulnus* of Christ as the place of mystical ecstatic union of the soul with its divine beloved."

[32]Carter Heyward, *Touching Our Strength: The Erotic as Power and the Love of God* (San Francisco: Harper and Row, 1989), p. 99.

[33]Rita Nakashima Brock, *Journeys by Heart: A Christology of Erotic Power* (New York: Crossroad, 1988), p. 25.

[34]Matter acknowledges this controversy in her introduction (p. 15) and by quoting feminist scholars. Heyward summarizes it clearly in her entry on "Eros" in *DFT*, p. 86.

[35]Roland Bainton's volumes, *Women of the Reformation in Germany and Italy* (Minneapolis: Augsburg, 1971) and *Women of the Reformation in France and England* (Minneapolis: Augusburg, 1973) are hardly feminist but still pretty much unsurpassed in their wealth of information. Bainton also completed a third volume, *Women of the Reformation from Spain to Scandinavia* (Minneapolis: Augsburg, 1977).

[36]Quoted in Bainton, *Germany and Italy*, p. 55.

[37]This story is recounted by Bainton and by Alice E. Walter, *Katherina Luther— Liberated Nun* (St. Louis: Clayton Publishing House, 1981).

[38]See, for instance, Charmarie Jenkins Blaisdell, "Calvin's Letters to Women: The Courting of Ladies in High Places," *Sixteenth Century Journal* 8/3 (1982), 67–84, and Bainton, *France and England*. I have also recounted briefly the ministry of early Reformed women in *"Grandes Dames,"* cited above.

[39]This phrase originates with Dagmar Lorenz, "Vom Kloster zur Küche: Die Frau vor und nach der Reformation Dr. Martin Luthers," in *Die Frau von der Reformation zur Romantik: Die Situation der Frau vor dem Hintergrund der Literatur- und Sozialgeschichte*, ed. Barbara Becker-Cantarino, Modern German Studies, 7 (Bonn: Bouvier Verlag Herbert Grundmann, 1980).

[40]These orders were part of the *Religionsgesprach* of 1525 and are recorded by Caritas in her *Denkwürdigkeiten*, a chapter of which is translated by Gwendolyn Bryant in Katharina M. Wilson, ed., *Women Writers of the Renaissance and Reformation* (Athens, Ga.: University of Georgia Press, 1987), 287–303. Details and quotations are from this excerpt.

[41]Jeanne de Jussie, *Le Levain du Calvinisme, ou Commencement de l'heresie de Geneve* (Geneva: Imprimerie de Jules-Guillaume Fisk, 1865). The book is untranslated, but an excerpt appears in Barbara MacHaffie, *Readings in Her Story: Women in Christian Tradition* (Minneapolis: Fortress Press, 1992), pp. 79–86. Jane Dempsey Douglass also gives a helpful summary with short excerpts in *Women, Freedom, and Calvin* (Philadelphia: The Westminster Press, 1985), pp. 98–101. Calvin first came to Geneva in 1536.

[42]Quotations here are from MacHaffie, *Readings in Her Story*, pp. 79–86.
[43]Ricoeur, *Interpretation Theory*.
[44]Ibid. Cf. Calvin's notion of the "inner testimony of the Holy Spirit."
[45]Marjorie Hewitt Suchocki, *In God's Presence: Theological Reflections on Prayer* (St. Louis: Chalice Press, 1996) and Roberta Bondi, *Memories of God: Theological Reflections on a Life* (Nashville: Abingdon Press, 1995).
[46]Suchocki, pp 27–28.
[47]Ibid., p. 106.
[48]Bondi, p. 83.
[49]Ibid., p. 89.

Conclusion

[1]I learned from Letty Russell what she learned from Rilke, that we are to "love the questions," *Growth in Partnership* (Philadelphia: Westminster Press, 1981), p. 163. Letty also thinks in circles, like many feminists. See *Church in the Round: Feminist Interpretation of the Church* (Louisville: Westminster/John Knox Press, 1993). The notion of "eccentricity" I must credit to my friend and colleague, Dr. Charles Allen.

[2]I have also learned much from my friend, Johanna W. H. Bos, who weaves together Scripture and theology and autobiography in her books, *Reformed and Feminist—A Challenge to the Church* (Louisville: Westminster/John Knox Press, 1991), and *Reimagining God: The Case for Scriptural Diversity* (Louisville: Westminster John Knox Press, 1995).

[3]I agree with Bos when she reminds us that there is more than one "Reformed tradition," *Reformed and Feminist*, p. 9.

[4]The first line of "God's Grandeur," by Gerard Manley Hopkins, 1895.

[5]Flannery O'Connor, in a memorable anecdote, recounts a late night conversation about the Eucharist with a group of *literati*, including Mary McCarthy, who said she thought of the host as the Holy Ghost, "He being the 'most portable' member of the Trinity." *The Habit of Being* (New York: Farrar, Straus, and Giroux, 1979), p. 125.

[6]LaCugna, *God for Us*. LaCugna wants to link the doctrine of God with the doctrine of salvation, a connection she believes has been lost in Trinitarian controversies. Her guiding principle is that "for Christian theology, the mystery of God can be thought of only in terms of the mystery of grace and redemption" (p. 2).

[7]Again, I cannot take credit for the term *christo-eccentrism*; I first heard it from Charles Allen.

Index